The Phonics Playbook

The Phonics Playbook

How to Differentiate Instruction
so Students Succeed

Alison Ryan

JB JOSSEY-BASS™
A Wiley Brand

For general information on our other products and services or for technical support, please contact our Customer Care Department within the United States at (800) 762-2974, outside the United States at (317) 572-3993 or fax (317) 572-4002.

Wiley also publishes its books in a variety of electronic formats. Some content that appears in print may not be available in electronic formats. For more information about Wiley products, visit our web site at www.wiley.com.

Library of Congress Cataloging-in-Publication Data Is Available:

ISBN 9781394197453 (Paperback)
ISBN 9781394197460 (ePDF)
ISBN 9781394197477 (ePub)

Cover Design: Wiley
Cover Image: Courtesy of Alison Ryan
Author Photo by Jenna Henderson

SKY10069178_031124

Contents

About the Author

Alison Ryan, MEd, has been working in education since 2005. Her favorite roles include classroom teacher, reading interventionist, literacy specialist, and director of curriculum and instruction. Alison's training includes a master's degree in literacy leadership, ESL endorsement, Orton-Gillingham training, and Structured Literacy coursework. Alison founded Learning at the Primary Pond, Inc., in 2012 to help other teachers implement highly effective, engaging literacy instruction.

Acknowledgments

I am incredibly grateful for the opportunity to write for Jossey-Bass.

Thank you to my wonderful team for helping me carry out the mission of Learning at the Primary Pond and find time in my schedule to write! Ingrid, thank you for your input on the presentation that ultimately sparked the idea for this text.

Thank you to the amazing educators who are a part of the Learning at the Primary Pond community. You inspire me!

Thank you to my parents for supporting me in my education and helping me develop as a writer.

And last but certainly not least, thank you to my husband for your continued love and support (and for always doing the dishes).

Introduction

It was back-to-school night, and I was busy greeting the families of my soon-to-be kindergarten students. A couple approached me and introduced themselves as Heidi's (not her real name) parents. "She's so excited for kindergarten," Heidi's mother told me. "And she's actually already reading, probably at a second- or third-grade level. We'll send a book to school with her so you won't have to worry about finding her something to read."

My eyes widened. A kindergartener reading at a second- or third-grade level? As a relatively new teacher, I hadn't experienced anything like this before. "Wow," I said to Heidi's mother. "That's amazing. Thank you for letting me know, and for sending the books!" I mentally filed this information away and continued greeting the other families.

On the first day of school, Heidi greeted me with enthusiasm and was ready to dive right into learning kindergarten procedures and expectations. And, just like her mother said, she arrived with a book to read, which she eagerly opened during quiet time. As the days and weeks went on, Heidi continued to impress me. Not only was she an avid, skilled reader but she was also incredibly articulate and seemed to possess the maturity of a much older child. I worried about Heidi feeling bored at school, but she seemed perfectly content to finish her work quickly and read the books she brought each week.

Heidi is an adult now, and I still think of her from time to time, even though I haven't seen her in years. I also can't help but feel a tinge of regret when I think back to her time with me in kindergarten. Although Heidi seemed to enjoy her days in my classroom, at that time, I didn't have the knowledge that I needed to adequately challenge her. Up until then, I'd only taught prekindergarten and kindergarten, and I didn't have a sense of what skills came next. As a result, I did not deliver the same quality of instruction to Heidi as I was able to provide to the other children who were working at a kindergarten level. Sure, I met with Heidi and discussed the books she was reading. My assistant and I added extra challenges for her within the daily work that all students completed. But did I *teach* her the skills she'd need to decode challenging multisyllabic words? Did I *instruct* her in how to use comprehension strategies to elevate her thinking? Unfortunately, the answer is no.

During our careers in education, I think most of us rack up a list of regrets like this, some big and some small. On our mental lists are the names of students we felt we could have helped more. Honestly, it makes sense that we feel this way! We chose teaching as a career because we want to make a difference in students' learning and in their lives. We take this job very seriously, and we want to do the best that we can.

I believe that the job of a teacher requires us to forgive and facilitate: to forgive ourselves for what we did not know or were not able to accomplish, but also to facilitate our own learning and growth. In my case, I needed to gain a deeper understanding of what phonics skills should be taught after kindergarten, how to teach students to decode multisyllabic words, and how to foster higher-level thinking skills. If I had only known then what I know now, I'm confident that I could have helped Heidi achieve more growth that year. At the same time, I forgive myself for my lack of knowledge. I can't go back in time and fix it. I choose to focus instead on what I *can* currently control: giving my current students (who now also include educators) the best instruction that I can.

All of this said, even when we do have the necessary knowledge to effectively support our students, there are still many aspects of teaching that are very much out of our control. For example, there were 24 other students in Heidi's class that year, including children who began school without any alphabet knowledge. The amount of time I could spend working individually with Heidi was always going to be limited, even if I had had more complete knowledge of how to help her. The confines of the school day, coupled with the fact that each teacher is only one person, mean that we will always be restricted in the amount of personalized attention we can give each individual student. This is the differentiation dilemma.

The Differentiation Dilemma

Many teachers struggle to effectively tailor their instruction to meet the individual needs of students (usually referred to as *differentiating*). Sometimes, this struggle results from a lack of knowledge about content, like in my story about Heidi. Sometimes, it stems from a lack of knowledge about practical strategies that make differentiation feasible for a busy teacher. Many times, however, this struggle is rooted in the limitations of the educational system itself.

Here's why: most schools are set up to "educate the masses" through standardized processes. Classroom teachers are given curricula to teach and sets of skills to cover. Regardless of what skills students have and have not yet mastered when they begin the school year, they will (for the most part) be taught the same content. Certainly, some parts of the school day are designed to meet students' unique needs (e.g., small-group instruction). Students who qualify for special education services are given extra support, or even different content to learn. Gifted students might also receive special instruction. However, the education system as a whole is not designed for fully personalized learning that takes into account the unique strengths and needs of each individual child. If it were, we would need far more than one teacher for every 20 to 30 (or more) students.

I point out this information not to discourage you from differentiating your instruction, nor to imply that the system is broken and there is no hope. Rather, I mention it because I want you to release yourself from the burden of any stress or guilt you might feel from not being able to do "enough" for your students. Many teachers are perfectionists in their instruction, and understandably so. We get to know our students and their academic needs very closely. After all, this is what we are told to do! However, once we are acquainted with students' needs, we naturally want to provide instruction that's just right for each student. But there's only one of us, and the large number of students we work with often have a wide range of needs. This can lead to feelings of frustration. Sometimes our own frustration can even leave us feeling a bit paralyzed. In the dark corners of our minds, we think, "This is impossible," because we can't personalize our instruction to the extent that we would like to. Instead of differentiating when we can, we feel inadequate and helpless, and our disempowerment leads us not to differentiate much at all. Or perhaps the opposite happens: we feel so much pressure that we try to differentiate every single minute of the school day! But that only leaves us feeling exhausted and ultimately leads to the realization that our current differentiation practices aren't sustainable.

If you struggle with differentiation, I'm here to tell you that you're not alone. You are, more than likely, working within a system that is not designed to support you in fully meeting all students' unique needs. However, when you have the knowledge and tools necessary to differentiate where and when it matters most, this leads to tremendously positive outcomes for your students. The information in this book will empower you to effectively differentiate in an extremely important skill area for young students: phonics instruction.

Why Differentiation Matters in Phonics Instruction

Phonics—instruction that teaches the relationships between letters and sounds—is an essential component of early literacy instruction (National Reading Panel, 2000). Phonics knowledge plays a key role in students' ability to decode (read) words. Being able to decode words helps build students' reading fluency. Fluent reading, in turn, contributes to reading comprehension (e.g., Fuchs et al., 2001). Phonics, therefore, serves as an important foundation of reading success. Plus, phonics knowledge contributes to students' spelling and writing abilities. Although writing involves many skills beyond correct spelling, being able to fluently spell words helps our students more easily get their thoughts onto paper.

Research on children's spelling and reading knowledge indicates that students tend to master phonics patterns in a relatively predictable order, but at different rates. This holds true even for students with diagnosed learning disabilities and dyslexia. (Bear et al., 2016). Picture a group of children proceeding up the same staircase (where each stair step is a set of phonics skills), but they are all standing on different steps on that staircase (see Figure I.1). In a third-grade classroom, for example, you might have some students still learning long vowels with silent *e*, while other students are learning to decode multisyllabic words with the *schwa* sound.

Our instruction needs to guide each student up the phonics staircase, one step at a time. Differentiating our phonics instruction helps us accomplish this. When we differentiate, we create opportunities for children to work on learning tasks that are just a little bit challenging. We provide teacher support so that students can be successful and eventually complete these once-challenging tasks on their own

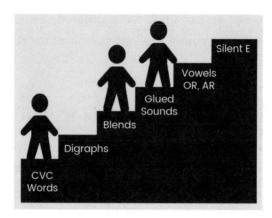

FIGURE I.1 The phonics staircase.

(to climb to the next phonics stair step). This concept of a "just right" level of difficulty for learning tasks (the zone of proximal development) was introduced by Vygotsky (1978) and has been supported by subsequent neuroscientific studies (Sousa & Tomlinson, 2018).

Knowing where a student's zone of proximal development is helps us avoid instructional activities that are far too difficult or easy. If a learning task is too difficult, students might experience a stress response, and their brains perceive the task as a threat (Sousa & Tomlinson, 2018). This, of course, can lead to a fight, flight, or freeze response, and it certainly does not lead to optimal learning. However, if a lesson or activity is too easy, students will not continue to advance in their learning. Additionally, if students perceive a task as too easy, the hippocampal memory system in the brain will identify it as something that has already been accomplished and as offering no novelty (Kumaran & Maguire, 2007). No novelty means that it is much less likely that dopamine will be released. A lack of dopamine means less focus, memory, and motivation, so you might notice students avoiding a too-easy task altogether (Sousa & Tomlinson, 2018).

To relate this to phonics instruction, let's say you're working with a child who hasn't fully mastered reading simple, three-letter words with short vowels. If you start teaching them to read long vowel words, the student isn't likely to be successful with this new skill; long vowels are typically mastered after students learn short vowels (Bear et al., 2016). However, if the student already knows all letter names and sounds, sticking exclusively to alphabet instruction would not sufficiently challenge them. For the student to make the most progress, you should stick with those three-letter words with short vowels (their zone of proximal development), rather than trying to push them up the phonics staircase before they are ready, or leaving them stuck at the bottom.

As we've discussed, it's usually not possible to differentiate instruction for every component of the school day. However, because phonics instruction plays such a crucial role in reading and writing, this is an area where we should differentiate as much as possible.

Where Do I Begin?

Now that we've discussed the importance of differentiating your phonics instruction, you might wonder, how do I start? Your first task is to understand where each student is currently standing on the staircase of phonics skills (their zone of proximal development). Only then can you select learning activities that are appropriate for their current stages of development. To gain this understanding of students' abilities and needs, it is necessary to assess your students. This is what we will explore in the first chapter.

After we dive into assessment, we'll discuss effective instructional practices and activities for teaching phonics (Chapter 2). Chapters 3 through 6 offer various models and approaches for differentiating your phonics instruction. I recommend reading Chapters 1 through 6 in order. Then, Chapters 7 and 8 will help you address the needs of specific groups of students (kindergarteners and English language learners); you can skip these chapters if they do not apply to you. The final chapter provides ideas for differentiated phonics activities that students can complete independently (e.g., in centers). Chapters 7 through 9 can be read out of order, at any point.

References

Bear, D. R., Invernizzi, M., Johnston, F. A., & Templeton, S. (2016). *Words their way: Word study for phonics, vocabulary, and spelling instruction*. Pearson.

Fuchs, L. S., Fuchs, D., Hosp, M. K., & Jenkins, J. J. (2001). Oral reading fluency as an indicator of reading competence: A theoretical, empirical, and historical analysis. *Scientific Studies of Reading, 5*(3), 239–256. https://doi.org/10.1207/s1532799xssr0503_3

Kumaran, D., & Maguire, E. A. (2007). Match–mismatch processes underlie human hippocampal responses to associative novelty. *The Journal of Neuroscience, 27*(32), 8517–8524. https://doi.org/10.1523/jneurosci.1677-07.2007

National Reading Panel. (2000). *Report of the National Reading Panel—teaching children to read: An evidence-based assessment of the scientific research. Literature on reading and its implications for reading instruction*. National Institute of Child Health and Human Development. https://www.nichd.nih.gov/sites/default/files/publications/pubs/nrp/documents/report.pdf

Sousa, D. A., & Tomlinson, C. A. (2018). *Differentiation and the brain: How neuroscience supports the learner-friendly classroom* (2nd ed.). Solution Tree Press.

Vygotsky, L. S. (1978). *Mind in society: The development of higher psychological processes*. Harvard University Press.

CHAPTER ONE

Assessing Students' Needs So You Can Differentiate

The term *assessment* can feel like a loaded word for teachers. Although assessments can be an excellent tool for learning about students' strengths and needs, assessments can also be time-consuming and difficult to administer while simultaneously managing a classroom. The good news, however, is that an assessment for purposes of phonics differentiation can be relatively quick and easy to administer. Our goal in giving this type of assessment is to determine which specific phonics skills a child has mastered, and which skills they have not yet mastered. With this information in hand, we can determine what's next for each child or where their zones of proximal development will be.

What Are We Looking For?

Before we discuss a specific assessment to guide you in differentiation, we need to be clear on what we are looking for when we assess. As we'll discuss in the next section, there are a variety of assessments available that can provide helpful insight into students' phonics abilities. However, when we are seeking to differentiate our phonics instruction, our primary goal is to determine which specific phonics skills a child can apply to decoding (reading) words, and which phonics skills a child can apply to encoding (spelling) words. For example, we want to determine if a

K–3 General Sequence of Phonics Skills

Consonant and short vowel sounds (alphabet)

Consonant-vowel-consonant (CVC) words and plural CVC words

Consonant digraphs

Double final consonants (-ff, -ll, -ss, -zz)

Consonant blends

Glued sounds

R-controlled vowels or, ar (er, ir, and ur might be taught for decoding but are not typically mastered until after students have learned vowel teams)

Silent e

Vowel teams

R-influenced vowel patterns (all vowels)

Diphthongs

Complex consonants (silent consonants, three-letter blends, soft c and g, word endings -dge/, -ge, and -tch/-ch)

Adding -ing and -ed to one-syllable words where the base word spelling changes

Unaccented syllables with schwa

Advanced prefixes and suffixes, including Greek and Latin roots

Note: Many students will not have fully mastered all of these skills on completing third grade. For a more detailed scope and sequence with additional skills, visit `fromsoundstospelling.com/book` and download ours for free.

child knows how to read and spell words with consonant digraphs so that we can provide instruction on consonant digraphs if needed.

If your school has provided you with a scope and sequence, or an ordered list of phonics skills to teach, you can use that resource to determine which specific skills you should assess. However, if you don't have a scope and sequence, or you're interested in seeing skills above or below your grade level sequence, refer to the included "K-3 General Sequence of Phonics Skills," which is based on developmental spelling research.

Remember, children might vary in the rate at which they learn these skills, but they will typically acquire these skills in largely the same order (Bear et al., 2016). Additionally, it is normal for children to have some gaps in their knowledge. Perhaps a skill was introduced, but a child did not fully master it at that time. Although they were able to continue learning more advanced skills, you will need to loop back and address the skill gaps so that they do not interfere with students' decoding and encoding.

Choosing the Right Phonics Assessment to Guide Differentiation

There are many different phonics and reading assessments available. Although we won't discuss all types of assessments in this chapter, we will look at some common types of assessments that many teachers are required to or choose to administer. Understanding the type and purpose of an assessment can help you determine whether it gives you an accurate representation of the information you are seeking.

Norm-Referenced Assessments

First, let's explore *norm-referenced assessments*. A norm-referenced assessment compares a student's skills or knowledge to that of their peers (a norm group). A norm group is typically made up of several thousand students in a state, region, or country. Norm-referenced assessments will often provide results in a percentile rank format. For example, a child's results on a reading assessment might indicate that they fall in the 30th percentile. This means that the child scored as well as or better than 30% of students in the norm group. The remaining 70% of students in the norm group scored higher than this student. Norm-referenced assessments can be helpful in identifying students who need special services because they have scored much lower than other students, or because they have scored much higher than other students. A percentile rank by itself does not, however, reveal whether a student is proficient with a set of specific skills.

One common type of norm-referenced test is a universal screener. A universal reading screener is designed to help educators quickly identify students who might have reading difficulties or are at risk of developing reading difficulties. Universal screeners are often given one to three times per academic year. Screeners are usually quick (e.g., students decode as many nonsense words as they can in one minute or read as many words of a passage as they can in one minute). These can alert you to students who might be struggling (or who are very advanced) by comparing them to a norm group. Universal screeners often indicate which students need to improve their fluency in terms of being able to produce letter sounds quickly, decode words quickly, or read texts quickly. However, universal screeners do not tell you which specific skills students have or have not mastered.

Criterion-Referenced Assessments

A *criterion-referenced assessment* compares students' skills or knowledge to specific standards or learning goals. For example, you might learn that a child got 75% of the questions about the main idea correct. The test results might also use a label like *proficient* to describe these results. A criterion-referenced assessment does not compare each student to other students. Instead, it focuses solely on predetermined academic goals, and it tells you if a student met those goals.

Many norm-referenced and criterion-referenced assessments will not give us the information we need in order to differentiate our phonics instruction. Although data from a norm-referenced assessment could help us see how a child performs in phonics in comparison to their peers, this does not tell us which specific phonics skills a child has and has not mastered. A criterion-referenced assessment that only gives us a score of *proficient* or *not proficient* is not helpful for this purpose, either. We need more detailed information about a child's mastery of specific phonics skills.

That said, some norm-referenced and criterion-referenced assessments do provide additional information about mastery of specific phonics skills. If you have assessment results that provide this information, you might already have what you need to differentiate. The results would need to show you, for example, that a student has mastered reading and spelling CVC words, digraphs, double final consonants, blends, and glued sounds, but not yet *r*-controlled or long vowels. If the assessment does not provide this level of specificity, it will not give you enough information to successfully differentiate using the strategies set forth in this text.

What type of assessment, then, do we need to administer so that we can effectively differentiate our phonics instruction? We need an informal *diagnostic* assessment. A diagnostic assessment tests students' skills and knowledge in specific areas. To determine which phonics skills students have and have not mastered, we can ask our students to read and spell lists of carefully selected words. For students who cannot yet read or spell words, we can instead assess their letter-sound knowledge. Note that other assessments that test related skills like phonemic awareness might also be helpful in guiding our reading instruction. However, for the purposes of this book, we are going to focus on phonics-specific assessments.

Administering a Diagnostic Phonics Assessment

Figure 1.1 shows a diagnostic phonics assessment, which you can access in the Appendix. In the first part of this assessment, you will have students read a list of words aloud to you. This should be done in a one-on-one setting, but it will not require more than a few minutes of dedicated

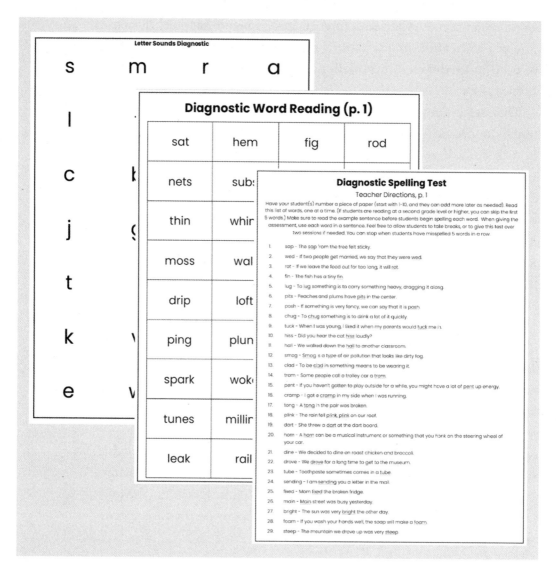

FIGURE 1.1 Diagnostic phonics assessment.

time per child. To save time, prepare the provided class scoring sheets or individual student scoring sheets prior to sitting down with a child. To begin this part of the assessment, sit at a table with the student results sheet, your scoring sheets, and a pencil. Place the first word list in front of the child you are assessing. You can start with the first set of words, or skip a few sets if you know that the child can easily decode them. Use a blank sheet of paper to cover up the columns of words that the child is not currently reading to help prevent visual overwhelm. Follow the script and directions provided in the Appendix to have the student read the words aloud to you. You can stop the assessment once the child misses five words in a row.

The second part of the assessment, the spelling test, can be given in a whole-class or small-group setting. Sometimes, it is easier to ensure that students are following along if you give this portion of the assessment in a small-group setting. Plus, in a small-group setting (especially if you create similar-ability groups), you can more easily discontinue after students misspell five words in a row. Either way, you'll want to make sure that students cannot see each other's papers as they work. Many teachers have students arrange folders in a standing-up position on their desks or tables, creating private work spaces for each student.

Students who are not yet reading (or who are only beginning to read CVC words) should be given the provided letter sounds assessment. In this assessment, you will sit one-on-one with each student and have them tell you the sound for each letter. Just like with the word reading assessment, you can use blank paper to cover up the letters that the child is not currently working on. If a student says a letter's name, say, "You said the letter's *name*. What's the *sound*?"

Optionally, you can also give a letter sounds spelling assessment. This should be given in a small-group or one-on-one setting. For this assessment, you'll say, "Number one is the sound /m/. Say /m/. Write a letter for /m/." Then, you'll give students time to spell the sound. This test can take a while to administer, especially with students who are just learning to form alphabet letters. Therefore, it is perfectly acceptable to skip this and instead use students' performance on the provided letter sounds assessment to guide your differentiation. You can observe students' abilities to spell letter sounds as you work with them over time.

Analyzing the Results

Once students have completed all parts of the assessment, it's time to use their results to determine what skills they have mastered and what they still need to work on. If you only tested students on their letter sounds and did not have them read or spell words, your completed class scoring sheet will reveal which letters students need to learn. When less than 60% of your class needs to learn a specific letter, this skill could be addressed in a small-group setting (more about this in Chapter 7). When 60% or more of your students missed a certain letter sound, you can work on this letter with all of your students. In Chapter 7, you'll learn strategies to challenge students who already know the letter that you're teaching.

If you gave the word reading and spelling tests provided in the Appendix, you'll already have filled out the word reading portion, but you will still need to complete the word spelling portion based on students' results. When filling in the word spelling portion, use a checkmark to indicate that a student spelled a word correctly. If they spelled the word incorrectly, note what they wrote instead (see Figure 1.2).

You'll notice that some words on each student results sheet have underlined portions. These underlined portions are designed to help you focus on the phonics feature that is being tested. If, for example, a child spells the word *swipe* as *sipe*, you'll see that the *i* and *e* are underlined, indicating that the child is demonstrating mastery of the target skill (silent *e*, in this case). You can make a mental note to continue working on blends with this student. Note that if a word does not have any underlining, the student must spell the word completely correctly in order to demonstrate mastery of the skill.

Once you have finished filling out all portions of the student results sheets, you will have a clear picture of the phonics skills that your students can apply to decoding and spelling words. Although no assessment is perfect (and a child can certainly have an off day), the results

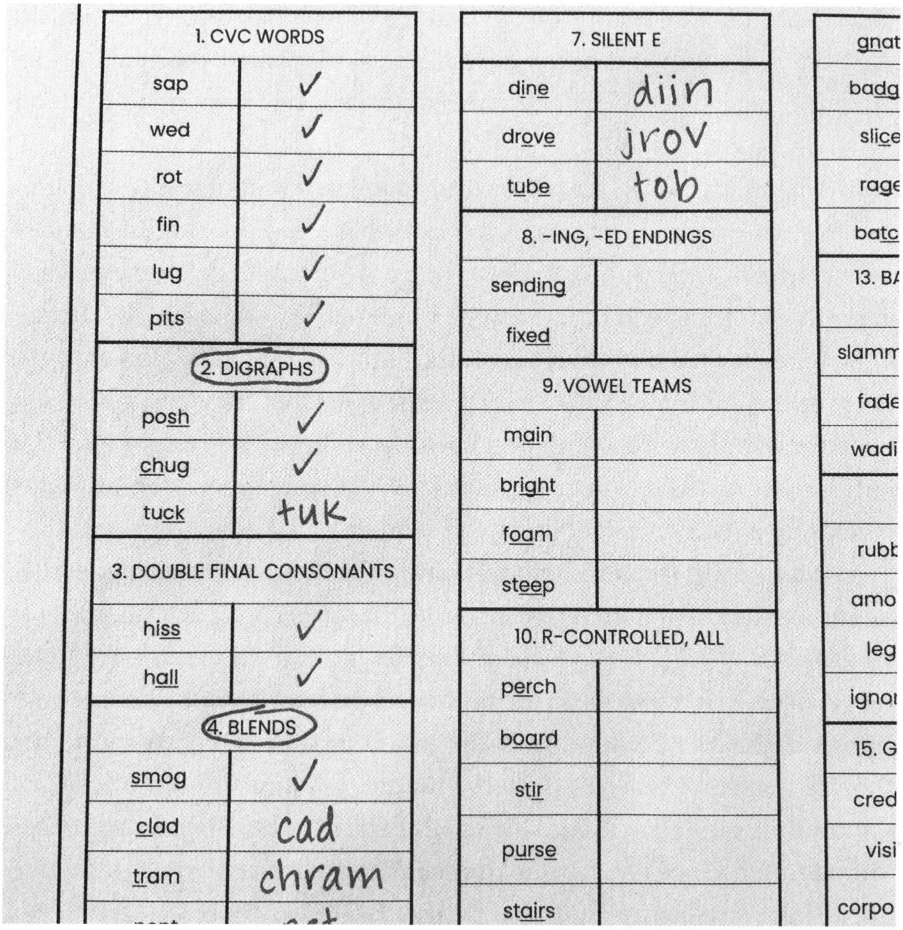

1. CVC WORDS			7. SILENT E			gnat
sap	✓		di̲ne	diin		ba̲dg
wed	✓		dr̲o̲ve	jrov		sli̲ce
rot	✓		t̲u̲be	tob		ra̲ge
fin	✓		8. –ING, –ED ENDINGS			ba̲tc
lug	✓		sendi̲ng			13. B/
pits	✓		fix̲e̲d			
2. DIGRAPHS			9. VOWEL TEAMS			slamm
po̲sh	✓		ma̲i̲n			fade
ch̲ug	✓		bri̲g̲ht			wadi
tu̲ck	tuk		fo̲a̲m			
3. DOUBLE FINAL CONSONANTS			st̲e̲ep			rubb
						amo
hi̲ss	✓		10. R-CONTROLLED, ALL			leg
ha̲ll	✓		pe̲rch			igno
4. BLENDS			bo̲a̲rd			15. G
sm̲og	✓		sti̲r			cred
cl̲ad	cad		pu̲rse			visi
tr̲am	chram		sta̲i̲rs			corpo

FIGURE 1.2 Scoring the spelling portion of the diagnostic phonics assessment.

from this diagnostic phonics assessment will serve as an excellent starting point for planning your differentiated instruction. If you are giving this assessment at the beginning of the school year, you might notice that certain skills need to be taught or retaught before you begin moving through your grade-level scope and sequence. Or you might find that you can skip certain skills in your scope and sequence, because students have already mastered them. You might also notice, when analyzing the results, that many students can decode more challenging words than what they can spell. This is normal. When choosing what skills to work on, you will want to begin with the skills that appear first on the sequence, regardless of whether those areas of need are related to students' decoding or spelling.

If you are teaching second or third grade, you might notice that your students have a few (or many) gaps in their knowledge, such as kindergarten or first-grade skills that they have not yet mastered. Some teachers worry that if they spend time teaching those "easier" skills, it will rob them of the time they need to cover second- or third-grade skills. However, it is worth spending time addressing those gaps so that they don't hold students back in their decoding and spelling abilities. You might also find that many students pick up on these skills relatively quickly, because they have likely already received instruction on them in previous grades.

After looking through your data from the diagnostic phonics assessment, you might wonder, "How can I possibly meet all my students' needs?" Knowledge is power, but knowledge can also feel overwhelming. This is where we need to return to the concept of good-enough differentiation. Although you likely won't be able to create individual phonics lessons for each and every student, you can still use intentional planning to guide each student up the staircase of phonics skills and address their zones of proximal development. In Chapters 3 through 6, we will cover practical options for meeting a range of student needs, including how to teach phonics in a whole-group setting and still differentiate.

Using the Diagnostic Test Results to Form Groups

In upcoming chapters, we will discuss how to use small-group instruction as a tool for differentiation. However, with our assessment data fresh on our minds, this is a good place to discuss how you might group students based on their performance on the diagnostic phonics assessment. You might want to skim this section now and bookmark it for later. You can return to it after you've read Chapters 2 through 6 and have a better idea of how you want to organize your classroom for differentiation.

Typing student results into a spreadsheet (or using the class composites found at FromSoundsToSpelling.com/book) can be helpful in forming groups. Using sticky notes is another handy strategy for grouping, because you can physically arrange and rearrange the notes. To use this strategy, write students' names at the top of a set of sticky notes (one per child). Below each child's name, write the first three skills in the sequence that they missed, regardless of whether they missed those skills on the word reading or word spelling portion of the assessment. Here's an example (see also Figure 1.3):

- Carlos read and spelled all CVC words correctly.
- Carlos misspelled a digraph word, but read all consonant digraph words correctly.
- Carlos read and spelled all double final consonant words correctly.
- Carlos made several mistakes in reading and spelling words with blends.
- Carlos made several mistakes in reading and spelling words with glued sounds.
- Carlos did not read or spell any *r*-controlled *a* or *o* words correctly, and his test was stopped shortly thereafter.
- Carlos's sticky note would have "digraphs," "blends," and "glued sounds" listed as the first three skills to target. (On the word reading assessment, the three skill areas where Carlos missed words were blends, glued sounds, and *r*-controlled *a* and *o*. However, we are sticking with the three easiest skills that Carlos missed between both assessments, which would be digraphs, blends, and glued sounds.)

Once you have your sticky notes prepared, you can physically manipulate them to form groups. Aim for no more than three groups total (more on this in Chapter 4). Your groups will likely not be perfect

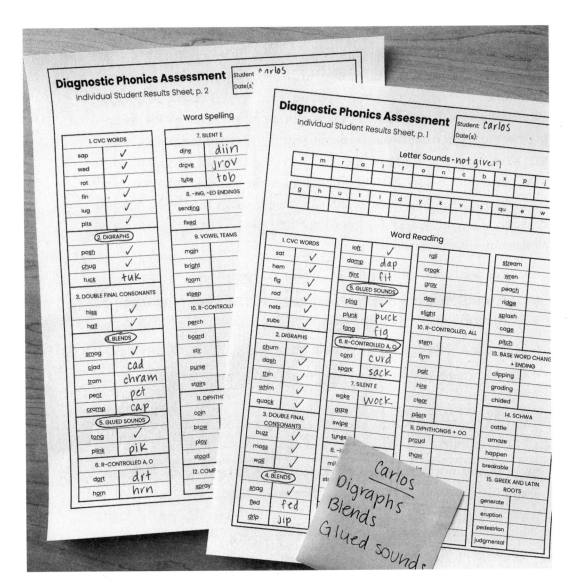

FIGURE 1.3 Carlos's results and sticky note.

matches, but try to find two areas of overlap (one at the least). For example, if Keisha missed consonant blends, *r*-controlled vowels *or/ar*, and silent *e*, and Megan missed *r*-controlled vowels *or/ar*, silent *e*, and vowel teams, both students could be placed in the same small group. However, if (in a separate example), Marcus missed consonant digraphs, double final consonants, and consonant blends, he would likely not do well in a group with Riley, who missed consonant blends, silent *e*, and vowel teams. In this example, Marcus still needs to work on many skills that Riley has already mastered.

Here are some additional points to consider when making groups:

- If you notice that many or all of your students missed a particular skill (e.g., double final consonants), you can plan to address it in a whole-group setting, even if you will be teaching other phonics skills in your small groups.

- Sometimes a student will miss a single word in a skill that falls earlier on the scope and sequence but then not make any other mistakes until later in the sequence. (For example, a child might miss a word with a glued sound but not make any other mistakes until she reached *r*-influenced vowels and diphthongs.) You might choose to make a mental note of that mistake but still place the child in a more advanced group, based on where most of her errors were made.

- It is common for students to be able to read harder words than what they can spell. When you are making groups, consider the easiest skills that a student missed, regardless of whether they missed those skills on the word reading or read spelling portions. (However, if you work with fluent readers, you can consider separating spelling and decoding instruction, which we discuss in Chapter 5.)

- Making groups is an art and a science! It's perfectly normal to create your groups and make changes later, once you've begun working with students.

- Use assessment data throughout the year to adjust your groups. You can use assessments from your curriculum or readminister the assessment in the Appendix midway through the year to evaluate student progress and adjust your groupings accordingly. However, you should also gather data on a weekly basis, as part of your routine phonics instruction (more on this in Chapter 2).

Remember, there's no such thing as "perfect" differentiation, and this applies to forming groups, too. You might wish you could have eight different phonics groups in your class, because students' needs vary widely! However, as you probably already know, it would not be practical to meet with eight different groups. In Chapter 4, we will discuss why (and how) to limit the total number of small groups.

What's Next?

Once you're clear on the phonics skills that each student needs to work on, the question becomes, "How do I make this work in my classroom?" Because no classroom (or teacher) is exactly alike, there's no one "correct" way to differentiate your phonics instruction. Instead, you can select one of three models for structuring (and differentiating) your phonics instruction. The three models are as follows:

- Whole-class phonics instruction with built-in differentiation
- Daily phonics-focused small groups
- Phonics instruction as part of reading-focused small groups

In Chapters 3–5, we'll discuss detailed examples of what each of the three models looks like, as well as the strengths and limitations of each model. We'll also get practical by looking at example schedules and suggestions for organizing your classroom for success. I encourage you to approach each of the three chapters with an open mind. Having read over the three models listed, you might already have an idea of what you'd like to implement in your classroom. However, once you read through the examples and details of each model, you might decide that another model would be easier to implement than you previously thought, or that you'd like to combine elements of multiple models.

Once you've learned about each model, we'll discuss, in Chapter 6, the best way to choose the model that's right for you and your students. You'll learn how to use student data to select a model and why you might want to change your model at some point during the school year.

If you teach kindergarten, keep in mind that the beginning of your school year will likely need to look a bit different than what's described in the models. But not to worry—Chapter 7 is just for you! In Chapter 7, we'll discuss how to teach the alphabet, and what differentiation might look like in a kindergarten classroom.

Last but not least, if you work with many English language learners, please know that the concepts shared throughout this book still apply to these students. In Chapter 8, we will discuss specific instructional strategies for English language learners. Even if you do not currently work with English language learners, you will still benefit from reading Chapter 8, because it explains tools that help all students develop vocabulary and language skills during your phonics instruction.

Reference

Bear, D. R., Invernizzi, M., Johnston, F. A., & Templeton, S. (2016). *Words their way: Word study for phonics, vocabulary, and spelling instruction*. Pearson.

Effective Phonics Instruction Within Any Model for Differentiation

When I was a classroom teacher and had an entire room to set up at the beginning of the school year, I would diligently start working weeks before school began. I'd make room on the shelves for students' new school supplies, create a seating chart, and label their cubbies. I'd organize my classroom library and create a lunch choice board. But you know what I'd almost always forget to prepare? My lesson plans for the first week of school! A day or so before we welcomed students, I'd suddenly remember that I needed to actually *do* something with my class—not just invite them into a well-organized classroom. Cue the last-minute scramble!

You're probably much more organized than I was, and this would never happen to you. Nevertheless, I share this story because it's easy to make a similar mistake when it comes to differentiating your phonics instruction. Just like I was so preoccupied with the *logistics* and *organization* of my classroom during back-to-school time, many teachers are primarily concerned about the logistics and organization of their phonics block: how many phonics groups they should have, what their schedule should look like, and how to fit everything in.

Organization is incredibly important so that your classroom runs smoothly. However, we shouldn't skip ahead to thinking about the logistical *hows* and completely forget the *what*. We have to get crystal clear on what effective phonics instruction looks like, as well as which instructional activities we should leverage. For this reason, before we dive into the three differentiation models, we're going to take a look at the most important, research-backed principles to follow for effective phonics instruction in any model. We'll also explore high-impact, engaging phonics routines that you can use on a daily and weekly basis. By the end of this chapter, you'll have a strong foundational understanding of the principles of effective phonics instruction, as well as learning activities that follow these principles so that you'll be ready to dive into differentiation logistics in subsequent chapters.

Research-Based Principles for Effective Phonics Instruction

Research in education (like any field), is always ongoing. However, some principles have been proven to be valid time and time again, by multiple studies. Here, we'll break down four of those important, research-based principles that should guide our phonics instruction.

Phonics Instruction Should Be Systematic

Exactly what effective phonics instruction looks like from classroom to classroom can vary. However, we do know that phonics instruction must be *systematic* (National Reading Panel, 2000). To teach phonics *systematically* means to follow a set scope and sequence. A phonics scope and sequence lists out the phonics skills that should be taught and in the order that they should be taught. For example, if you're teaching first grade, your scope and sequence would guide you to cover words with short vowels before you teach long vowel words.

Systematic seems like a simple concept, right? But phonics is not always taught this way. In some approaches, phonics skills are taught *incidentally*. For example, if a teacher happens to choose a story for students that contains many long *e* words, she might decide to teach long *e* patterns at that time. Her decision to teach this phonics skill is not based on a scope and sequence; rather, the skill was chosen based on a text. This approach is not what the research indicates will result in the best outcomes for student learning. You might wonder, "What if a story I read with my students *does* have a lot of long *e* words? Should I talk about those words at all?" The answer is *yes*, absolutely! As we'll discuss in the upcoming section "Students Need Out-of-Context Instruction, as Well as In-Context Instruction," we want students to make connections between phonics skills and the texts they're reading. When you read that story, by all means, take some time to have students find long *e* words, discuss how they're spelled, and so on. What we *don't* want to do is rely on texts (or random selection) to guide our choice of phonics skills to teach during our core lessons. Instead, we want to use a scope and sequence, progressing through the list of skills in order. That's systematic phonics instruction, and it will help our students learn more effectively than if we used incidental phonics instruction.

Phonics Instruction Should Be Explicit

The research also indicates that phonics instruction should be *explicit* (National Reading Panel, 2000). Explicit phonics instruction involves intentionally teaching students the relationships between *graphemes* and *phonemes*.

Let's break down these two terms:

- *Phoneme:* a single sound; the smallest unit of speech (you might see these written with slash marks, like this: /m/, /sh/, /ē/)

- *Grapheme:* a letter or combination of letters that represent a phoneme (examples: *m, sh, ea*)

Some graphemes represent more than one phoneme in English. For example, the grapheme *s* can represent the /s/ sound in words like *sun* and the /z/ sound in words like *nose*.

Now let's return to the concept of *explicit*. In explicit phonics instruction, we teach students that, for example, the vowel pattern *oa* can represent the long *o* sound. You might hold up a card with *oa* on it and explain that the two vowels are working together, as a team, to represent the long *o* sound. Then, you would have students apply this knowledge to read and spell words with *oa*.

You can contrast this approach with *implicit* phonics instruction. In implicit phonics instruction, students are expected to draw conclusions about phonics patterns simply from reading (or seeing the teacher read) whole words. Instead of teaching students about *oa* as described, you might ask students if they can figure out what sound the *oa* pattern represents when you happen to encounter an *oa* word in text. Or you might expect students to infer this information simply by attempting to read *oa* words that are part of a text, without support. Explicit phonics instruction, however, does not rely on students to figure out phoneme-grapheme connections on their own.

There is more to explicit instruction than how we teach grapheme-phoneme relationships, however. As Vaughn and Fletcher (2021) explain in their article "Explicit Instruction as the Essential Tool for Executing the Science of Reading," explicit instruction also requires teachers to break down complex skills into smaller tasks, use modeling and think-alouds during instruction, provide corrective feedback to students, distribute practice over time, and have students revisit previously taught skills. Explicit instruction also requires teachers to use assessment data and their understanding of students' current strengths and weaknesses to create appropriate learning opportunities for students. Read the Case Study on the next page for an example of how a teacher might use these features of explicit instruction to teach students how to decode and spell words with consonant blends.

In this example, we see that Mr. Brown broke down a skill (consonant blends) into manageable chunks; he had students begin working with just two types of blends. He used modeling and a think-aloud to demonstrate to students how to decode words with blends by adding

CASE STUDY

Mr. Brown plans a lesson where he will introduce the concept of consonant blends. Instead of asking students to work with many kinds of words with blends, he starts with initial *s*-blends *st* and *sp* (like in the words *stop* and *spin*).

During this first lesson, Mr. Brown introduces the concept of a blend. He models, with several words, how to blend the first two sounds in a word, then add the vowel and final consonant sound (/s/ /t/, /st/, /ĕ/, /stĕ/ /p/). He explains that blending just two sounds at a time can make it easier to put the sounds together. Next, students help him decode a few more *st* and *sp* words. Mr. Brown notices that students are doing well with the new concept, so he feels comfortable continuing on to have them spell words with *st* and *sp*. He gives students sound box strips as a tool to

help them with segmenting. With his support, students use magnetic letters to segment and spell various words that begin with the blends *st* and *sp*. He helps students notice and correct their mistakes.

Over the next days and weeks, Mr. Brown continues to add additional blends (*s*-blends, *l*-blends, *r*-blends, and different types of ending blends) for students to decode and spell. He uses decodable texts that focus on blends to have students apply what they are learning to their reading. He also makes sure that students practice reading and spelling digraph words, because their previous phonics unit focused on digraphs. At the end of each week, Mr. Brown gives students a dictation (similar to a spelling test) to help guide his lessons during the following week.

just one sound at a time. As students completed the assigned tasks (e.g., spelling words with blends), Mr. Brown gave feedback so that they could correct and learn from their mistakes. Mr. Brown provided instruction on this skill set through brief lessons that took place over multiple weeks (distributed practice), and he will continue to give students opportunities to work with consonant blends, even when the class moves on to the next phonics unit. He also made sure to review previously taught skills (digraphs, in this example) while working on blends. Mr. Brown effectively leveraged all areas of explicit instruction in order to help his students master phonics skills.

The research indicates that explicit phonics instruction is highly effective and leads to improved reading skills in students. We will continue to revisit the elements of explicit instruction throughout this book.

Students Need Out-of-Context Instruction, as Well as In-Context Instruction

This concept could be classified as part of explicit instruction, but it is so crucial to teaching phonics effectively that it deserves its own section! *Out-of-context phonics instruction* involves having students work with patterns (like *sh*, *oa*, etc.) and individual words. Mr. Brown's out-of-context phonics instruction included having students read and spell individual words with *st* and *sp*. Out-of-context phonics instruction helps students solidify their understanding of the relationships between phonemes and graphemes.

Students also need many opportunities for *in-context phonics instruction*. This type of phonics instruction or review is related to a text that you and/or the students are reading or writing. For example, after Mr. Brown introduced certain types of blends, he had students read decodable texts with those blends. A decodable text is a story, passage, or other text where the words are restricted to include only phonics patterns and high-frequency words that students have already been taught. Decodable texts are usually written to incorporate many words with a specific, target phonics skill (e.g., *s*-blends), so they're an excellent tool for in-context phonics practice. When it comes to writing, however, in-context phonics instruction looks a little different. Sometimes you might ask students to write sentences or paragraphs with the words you're working on during phonics instruction. Additionally, as you're writing in front of students during your daily writing lessons, you'll want to think aloud and model how you use phonics knowledge to spell words. For example, you might intentionally incorporate two words with *s*-blends in your modeled writing example. Later, you might have students reread their own writing and look for examples of *s*-blends and any other blends that they used to spell words.

In-context phonics instruction is important because it shows students how to apply their phonics learning to real reading and writing tasks.

Our ultimate goal in teaching phonics is to help students use that knowledge to read and write, so it's essential that we give students opportunities to do just that.

Students Need to Acquire General and Specific Word Knowledge

The English language is full of patterns. For example, the words *hat*, *lap*, and *jab* all contain the short *a* sound spelled with the letter *a*. Here's another example: the words *loud*, *spout*, and *proud* all contain the same diphthong vowel sound, spelled by *ou*. This is good news for a few reasons. First, if we had to teach students how to read and write every single word in the English language (hundreds of thousands of words, and counting), this would be a nearly impossible task. Second, the human brain seeks out patterns (Mattson, 2014), so students are naturally primed to learn and apply patterns to read and spell words.

What does this have to do with *general* and *specific* word knowledge? *General* word knowledge (as it relates to phonics learning) is knowledge of phonics patterns. We build students' general word knowledge when we teach them about short *a*, or the *ou* diphthong. Our goal is for students to use this general word knowledge to read and write many, many words, not just the particular words that we happen to include in our lessons. *Specific* word knowledge, however, is knowledge of how to spell individual words. For example, the word *seat* could potentially be spelled as *seet* (like *feet*). There is more than one way to spell the long *e* sound, so students need to acquire the specific word knowledge that seat is spelled *s-e-a-t*.

When it comes to our phonics instruction, we need to plan opportunities for students to acquire both general and specific word knowledge (Bear et al., 2016). Both are important and deserve instructional time. To teach general word knowledge, we focus on patterns and rules. We want to give students opportunities to generalize what they're learning, so we should ask students to read and spell words that we haven't specifically taught. We might, for example, give a spelling assessment at the end of the week that includes a few words that students aren't familiar with yet so that we can determine if they're able to apply the week's general word instruction to spell new words with the same pattern(s).

To build specific word knowledge, we need to teach students specific words. Because our time is limited, we should be intentional about choosing those words. Highly useful words, those which appear often in texts, should take priority. For example, we elect to spend more time on the word *boat* than we do on the word *loam*, because *boat* is a more useful word (it appears more frequently). We should also intentionally spend time on words that are irregularly spelled, as well as words like *seat* that contain sounds that could be spelled a few different ways.

Why Routines?

These best practices can guide us in choosing daily and weekly routines for our phonics instruction. A routine is simply a sequence of activities that you follow on a regular basis, and you probably already have many routines established in your classroom. For example, when teaching writing, you might consistently begin with a mini-lesson, provide time for students to practice while you meet with them individually and in small groups, and then finish up your writing block with time for students to share their work. This is a routine because you follow this structure most of or all of the time when teaching writing.

Phonics routines are helpful for a variety of reasons.

Routines Help with Behavior Management

Think back to a time when you held a classroom party or went on a field trip with students. Do you recall that some students' behavior on those days was less than ideal? If you haven't started teaching or you simply haven't experienced this yet, you'll likely discover that some students struggle to adapt to changes in your routines, even when the change is for something special and fun. Although breaking our routines is sometimes necessary (and enjoyable), regularly following set procedures can help students feel safe. Students know what to expect and are therefore more likely to adhere to our rules and expectations.

Routines Help Us Maximize Instructional Time

When you're teaching students how to do something new, it takes time for them to learn your expectations. There's the time spent explaining (and re-explaining) the new activity, plus time spent correcting or redirecting students as they learn what to do. However, when we stick to a handful of high-impact routines during our phonics instruction, we save time because we're not constantly explaining new activities. Routines also have the benefit of minimizing behavior interruptions, as we discussed in the previous section, and that further maximizes the amount of time we have available for instruction and student practice.

Routines Free Up Our Time and Energy so We Can Focus on Differentiation

Routines save you time when you're lesson planning, allowing you to spend more time determining how to meet students' individual needs. To make this more concrete, let's compare two teachers and their planning habits.

Teacher A has assigned specific phonics routines to each day of the week. For example, on Mondays, she teaches a mini-lesson on a new phonics pattern. She shows students a poster of the new pattern and discusses how the letters connect to the sounds (example: with the *ar* pattern, the "bossy" *r* changes the sound of the letter *a*). Then she has students blend to read a few words with that phonics pattern; she arranges stacks of the letter cards that she uses all year long. Next, students each take out a paper plate with colored sand for some quick *multisensory* practice with the phonics patterns they've been working on recently.

Last, students use magnetic letters to build words with the day's new phonics pattern. Teacher A knows that this is what most Mondays will look like all year long. She doesn't spend much time preparing materials for the lesson, because most of the activities use resources (letter cards, paper plates with sand, magnetic letters) that she already has and students know how to use. Teacher A follows a similar structure for the other days of the week, although the actual activities vary by day. She usually changes the routine only if she notices that students' needs require her to do something different.

Teacher B, however, prefers less structure in her phonics block. To introduce a new skill, she might find a video online, use a poster, bring in props, or create a digital slide deck. To have students practice reading words, she sometimes looks online for a word list, creates digital slides, or prepares a partner game. To have students practice spelling words, she might have them use magnetic letters, search online for a worksheet for them to complete, or try to find an app or website for practice. Each week, Teacher B spends quite a bit of time thinking about what activities she'd like to incorporate into her phonics block the following week, and even more time searching for and preparing materials for those activities.

In these examples, both Teacher A and Teacher B provide effective, engaging phonics instruction to their students. However, Teacher B spends significantly more time planning and preparing for her lessons, so she has less time to plan how she will differentiate instruction to meet a range of student needs. You might wonder, "Isn't it boring for the students in Teacher A's class to do the same activities repeatedly throughout the year? Wouldn't Teacher B's students have more fun?" Variety and novelty are certainly important in keeping students engaged. Nevertheless, it's possible to save time by sticking to routines and still provide variety within those routines. For example, Teacher A might change out the multisensory material from sand to baggies filled with colored hair gel. (Instead of tracing letters in sand, students trace a finger on top of the closed bag, creating an outline of the letter(s).) Or once a month,

Teacher A might introduce a new skill with an engaging video rather than by following her usual procedures. Following routines does not mean leaving the fun out of teaching and learning!

High-Impact Routines for Teaching and Practicing Phonics Skills

Now that we've discussed the value of routines, let's examine some actual activities that you might incorporate into your phonics block on a regular basis. Remember, research indicates that there is no one best way to teach phonics. Approach these routines as a helpful starting point, knowing that you can make adjustments as needed for your own preferences and for your students.

We will explore each of the following routines:

- New skill introduction
- Blending drill
- Word list reading
- Word sorts
- Decodable texts
- Word building
- Written dictation
- High-frequency word instruction
- Phonological awareness practice

New Skill Introduction

On certain days, you'll need to introduce a new phonics skill, pattern, or concept to your students. Depending on the level of your students, this new topic could be something like this: the name and sound of the letter *Gg*, the vowel team *ee*, or how to decode multisyllabic words with open and closed syllables using the V/CV rule. (These are explained in the lists that follow.) Your phonics scope and sequence (download one for free at `fromsoundstospelling.com/book`), as well as students' ability levels, will guide you in determining which skill to introduce next.

The way you introduce a new skill might vary somewhat, depending upon the nature of the skill that you're teaching. Here are some examples of how each skill is introduced in *From Sounds to Spelling*, the phonics program I authored:

Letter *Gg*

- Show students the letter on the classroom alphabet chart. Tell students the name and sound of the letter.

- Read students a brief rhyme that includes many words that begin with the letter *Gg*. Have students help you locate some of these words.

- Ask students to brainstorm some additional words that begin with the /*g*/ sound.

- Show students a "Letter Gg" video clip to teach them a chant that includes the name, sound, and movement for the letter.

- For context: this skill introduction sequence is followed by a picture sort, where students practice distinguishing between pictures that begin with the /*g*/ sound and pictures that do not begin with the /*g*/ sound. The next day, students focus on learning how to correctly write the letter *Gg*. During that lesson, students practice tracing the Letter *Gg* in sand or another sensory material, as well as writing the letter using pencil and paper.

Vowel Team *Ee*

- Display a poster with the letters *ee* and a picture of a tree. Explain that when two *e*s are next to each other in a word, they usually make the long *e* sound, /*ē*/. Have students repeat the sound.

- Ask students to brainstorm any words they know that have *ee* in them.

- Have students use sand or another sensory material to practice tracing and saying aloud, "*ee* says /ē/." (You can have students use the sensory material to review a few additional sounds.)

- For context: after the skill introduction, students practice blending to read words with *ee* and building words with *ee*. The next day, they read a decodable text with *ee* in addition to completing other activities to reinforce this concept.

Decoding Multisyllabic Words with Open and Closed Syllables

- Briefly review the concept of open and closed syllables (these skills have been taught previously).

- Write the word *robot* on the board. Ask students to identify the vowels in the word.

- Model how to circle the vowels and underline the consonant between the vowels (*b*).

- Display a poster for the V/CV rule. Explain that if there is only one consonant sound between the vowels, we can try dividing the word before the consonant.

- Model how to divide up the word like this: *ro/bot*.

- Ask students if the first syllable is open or closed (open, because it ends with a vowel) and have them identify the vowel sound (/ō/).

- Ask students if the second syllable is open or closed (closed; it ends with a consonant and has just one vowel) and have them identify the vowel sound (/ŏ/).

- Have students help you read each syllable and the entire word.

- Repeat this process with another word.

- For context: after the skill introduction, students practice dividing up additional words with open and closed syllables, using the V/CV pattern. Students also read a decodable text with more V/CV words.

As you can see from these examples, the way you introduce a skill depends entirely on what the skill is. Nevertheless, your plan for a skill introduction need not vary dramatically, especially when you are teaching related skills. For example, when you teach additional vowel teams (like *oa*), you can use the same process that you used to introduce *ee*. When you introduce a skill, keep your instruction brief and remember that students will not completely master the skill in those few short minutes. As students begin to apply the skill (e.g., by reading and writing words), their understanding of the concept will continue to grow.

Blending Practice

Once students have been introduced to a new phonics pattern, we want them to practice applying that pattern to read words. When we have students *blend*, we have them decode words by putting together the sounds in a word. For example, to read the word *chat*, students could say, "/ch/ /ă/ /t/, chat" (the letters within the slashes represent phonemes, or speech sounds).

Blending Drill

A blending drill is a simple routine that can be used for blending practice. In the version of the blending drill that we use in our phonics program, *From Sounds to Spelling*, the teacher displays stacks of letter cards to spell out a word (see Figure 2.1) The only sounds and patterns shown on the cards are ones that students have already been taught. If you have not yet taught the *sh* digraph, for example, you would not include that in the stacks of letter cards for the drill.

To begin the blending drill, the teacher points underneath each letter, one at a time, and students chorally say each sound, then the entire word: "/sh/ /ĕ/ /l/, shell." Students are not permitted to simply call out the word. Letters that work together to represent a single sound (*s-h* representing /sh/ and *l-l* representing /l/) are shown on a single card. This helps reinforce the idea that even though students see multiple letters,

FIGURE 2.1 Blending drill, first word.

FIGURE 2.2 Blending drill, second word.

those letters are working together to represent a single sound. Next, the teacher removes the top card from any one of these stacks to reveal a new word (in this example, *tell*; see Figure 2.2). The new word might be a real word, or it might be a *nonsense word*, a word that follows English spelling patterns but is not an actual word. You'll want to arrange the cards so that students are reading real words the vast majority of the time.

If you work with beginning readers, you might assume that you should not begin the blending drill until students know all their letters and can read *CVC words* (*consonant-vowel-consonant words*, the words students typically learn to read first) independently. However, this is not the case! You can begin modeling the blending drill as soon as students know three to five letter sounds. Instead of pointing to each letter while students say each sound and blend, you will use a three-step gradual release approach. First, you'll model how to say the sounds and blend to read the word. Second, you'll have students say the sounds and blend along with you. Third, you'll ask students to say the sounds and blend on their own. It will go like this:

Teacher: (sliding finger underneath the letter cards):
Listen while I say the sounds and blend to read this word: /mmm/ /ăăă/, /mă/, /t/, mat. Now let's do it together.

Teacher and Students: /mmm/ /ăăă/, /mă/, /t/, mat.

Teacher: Good! Now I'll point to each letter and you do it without me.

Students: /mmm/ /ăăă/, /mă/, /t/, mat.

Teacher: Great job! What word did you read?

Students: Mat!

Teacher: Right! The preschooler took a nap on his mat.

Here are a few points to notice from this example:

- The teacher and students pushed the sounds together smoothly (/mmm/ /ăăă/) rather than saying each sound individually and separately (/m/ /ă/). This strategy can be helpful for beginning readers or students who struggle with decoding.

- The teacher modeled a strategy referred to as *successive blending*, sometimes called *continuous blending*. In successive blending, the reader blends just two parts of the word at a time. For example, in the word *mat*, the teacher and students first put the sounds of the letters *m* and *a* together and said "/mă/" before adding the /t/ sound at the end. This strategy is especially helpful for students who are first learning to blend or who are struggling with blending.

- The word *mat* was chosen with intention. First, students had already been taught the sounds for all three letters: *m, a, t*. Second, *mat* begins with a *continuous* sound, /m/. A continuous sound is one that is produced with a nonstop flow of air. To understand this concept, try saying the sound of the letter *m* aloud for five seconds. Now try saying the sound of the letter *t* aloud for five seconds. Did you notice how you were able to produce the /*mmmm*/ sound continuously, while the /*t*/ sound stopped? The continuous sounds for the letters *a, e, f, i, l, m, n, o, r, s, u, v, w, y*, and *z* are usually easier for beginning readers to blend with when compared to stop sounds (like the sounds for the letters *d, g*, and *t*, for example). When students are first working on reading simple words, start with words that begin with continuous sounds like *mat*.

In the example of the blending drill with *mat*, you probably noticed that students are given a high level of support. You might wonder, "Why would I bother doing this if students are only able to read a word with so much help from me?" This is a great question to explore! First, seeing how letters are used to make words helps students master the *alphabetic principle*. The alphabet principle is the understanding that letters, which represent speech sounds, can be combined to make words. The alphabetic principle is essential for students to grasp so that they learn to decode words (Baker et al., 2018). Second, the blending drill builds letter-sound fluency because students are asked to produce sounds for letters as part of the drill. Third, watching and listening to you blend during this activity helps students master the skill of blending. Therefore, the three-step gradual release process is a temporary and beneficial scaffold that helps students eventually learn to decode words on their own.

If you find that students are still struggling with the blending drill, even with your help, consider starting with two-sound *VC (vowel-consonant) words* like *an, at, Ed, if, in, it, on, up, us*. VC words are a great starting place for beginning readers, especially when they begin reading words without your support. If you'd like to try the blending drill with your students, you can download a free set of cards that includes consonants, vowels, and vowel patterns at `https://www.fromsoundstospelling.com/book`.

Word Lists
You can also use a simple list of words to practice blending! See Figure 2.3 for an example from Level 1 of *From Sounds to Spelling*. Students begin with *made, take*, and then continue reading down each column. Notice

<table>
<tr><td colspan="3">**Long A CVCe Words Practice**
Wk 23 Lvl 1</td></tr>
<tr><td>made</td><td>safe</td><td>brave</td></tr>
<tr><td>take</td><td>skate</td><td>grapes</td></tr>
<tr><td>make</td><td>game</td><td>shape</td></tr>
<tr><td>late</td><td>chase</td><td>plates</td></tr>
<tr><td>came</td><td>state</td><td>waves</td></tr>
</table>

FIGURE 2.3 List of words for blending.

how the first several words contain fewer letters and sounds (so that they are easier for students to read). The words gradually increase in difficulty to include more complex patterns like digraphs and blends (e.g., the blend *sk* in *skate*, or the digraph *ch* in *chase*). For an extra challenge, some plurals are also included (*grapes* and *waves*). Even though the letters aren't placed on individual cards like in the blending drill, the task remains the same: students say each sound individually and blend to read the word (example: /m/ /ā/ /d/, *made*). Again, there are no words included that contain sounds or patterns that students haven't yet been taught.

Word Sorts

Word sorts are another great tool that help students apply their phonics knowledge to reading words. As we discussed previously in this chapter, it is important for students to acquire general word knowledge by learning about the patterns in words. Word sorts not only provide students with an opportunity to practice reading words but also they help students attend to word patterns.

In Figure 2.4, you'll see an example from Level 2 of *From Sounds to Spelling*. In this sort, students compare words that contain the /or/ sound in them. They are learning about the different ways to spell this

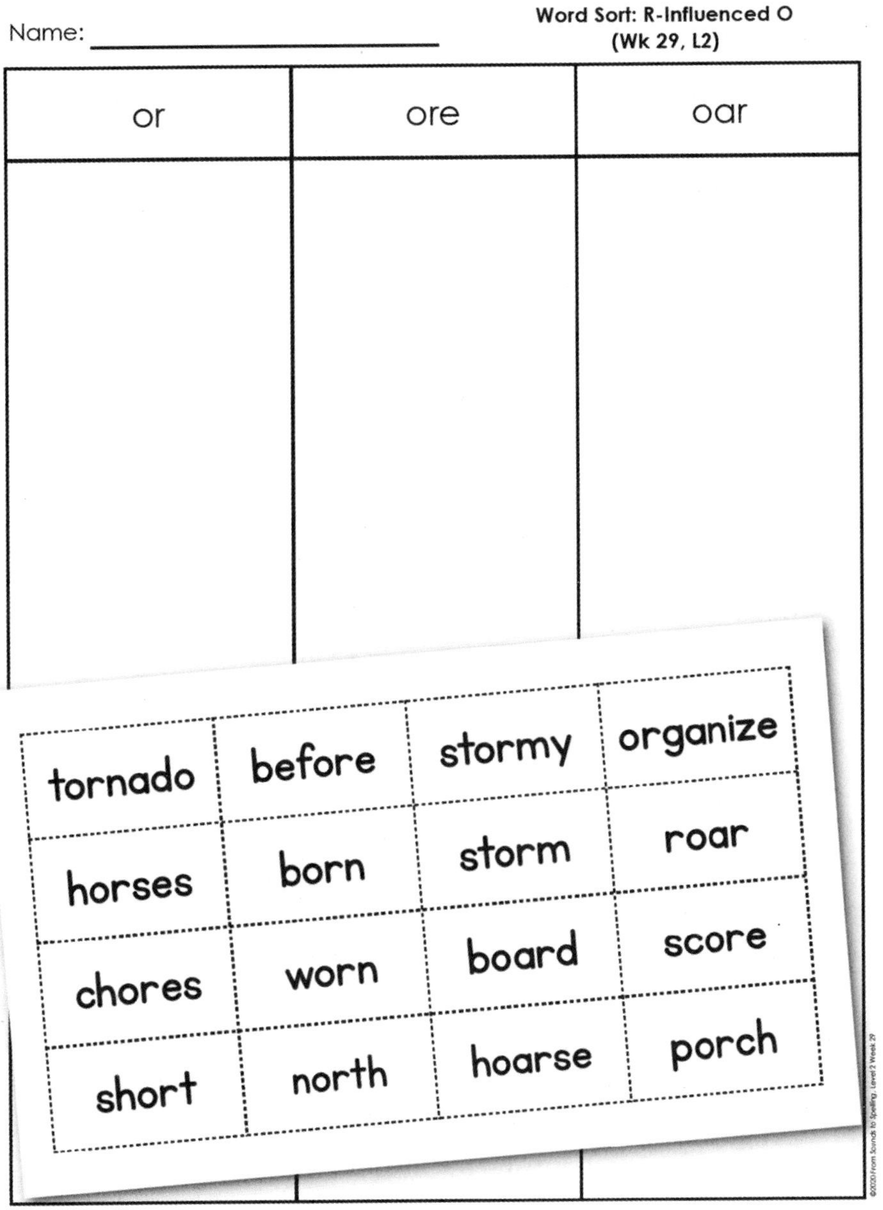

Name: _____

Word Sort: R-Influenced O
(Wk 29, L2)

or	ore	oar

tornado | before | stormy | organize

horses | born | storm | roar

chores | worn | board | score

short | north | hoarse | porch

FIGURE 2.4 Word sort example.

sound: *or*, *ore*, and *oar*. The sort helps reinforce the general word knowledge that the *or* sound can be spelled these three ways, and it also helps students acquire specific word knowledge as they see how the individual words in the sort are spelled.

To introduce a word sort, you'll want students to decode the words. This might be done chorally (as a group), or students might work in partners. You should also discuss the meaning of any words that might be unfamiliar to the students. For example, a teacher might explain the meaning of the word *hoarse* in the /or/ example sort. Next, students work independently or with a partner to cut apart and sort their words. As a student places a word in the correct column, they read the word again. Once all the words are sorted, they read the words a third time, this time by reading down each column. Although the word cards can be glued down, it's helpful to have students place them in a baggie or container after they are finished sorting. This way, students can practice sorting their words multiple times. For variety, students might time themselves reading and sorting their words, and then repeat the activity to see if they can beat their previous time.

Another related activity (that involves writing rather than reading) is what we call a *sort and write* in *From Sounds to Spelling*. In a sort and write, students create or are given blank paper with columns for each pattern. In our example, students would have blank paper labeled with three columns: one for *or*, one for *ore*, and one for *oar*. The teacher reads a word aloud to students, and students must decide which column the word goes in, plus spell that word correctly. For example, if the teacher reads the word chore aloud, students would write the word in the *ore* column. A sort and write is most successful after students have already had some practice decoding and spelling the words.

Decodable Texts

Reading individual words is certainly important in helping students learn to apply phonics skills. However, as students are developmentally ready, we also want them to read entire sentences and texts that contain examples of the phonics patterns they are learning. Decodable texts (sometimes called *decodables*, *decodable books*, or *phonics readers*) are a helpful tool that give students an opportunity to apply their knowledge to read connected text.

When selecting decodable texts, you'll want to look carefully at the types of words that are included. Most decodable texts focus on a specific phonics pattern or group of patterns (e.g., short *o* words, or silent *e* words). They also contain common high-frequency words. Figure 2.5 shows a decodable text that focuses on the *-op* word family (e.g., *mop, hop, shop*). The teacher is directed to pre-teach the words *gets*, and *Carlos*, because those are the only words that include phonics patterns that students haven't yet been taught. Students can decode all other words or recognize them as high-frequency words they have practiced. Figure 2.6 pictures a decodable text for practicing multisyllabic words with long *a* (e.g., *subway, pancake*). Students have been taught all high-frequency words included in the passage, as well as how to decode the other words, with the exceptions of *says* and *giggle*, which the teacher should pre-teach.

Some decodable texts will target a specific phonics pattern (e.g., *sh*) and include many words with this skill, but they also include words that are too advanced. For example, a decodable text on *sh* could include the word *shout*. Most students would not be able to decode the *ou* pattern in this word. Developmentally speaking, students do not master this tricky diphthong sound until much later, so it doesn't make sense to include this word in a book that targets *sh*.

This is why it's important to find decodable texts that largely match the scope and sequence of phonics skills that you're using with your students. Although it's perfectly acceptable to use a text that contains a few words that students might not know how to decode yet, we want to avoid having students practice phonics skills using texts that contain many words that are out of reach. The purpose of using decodable texts is to get students to apply their learning and gain experience (and

Name:	Skill: -op Word Family	Words to Pre-teach: gets, Carlos

Jack and the Duck

Jack gets a job.

Quick, Jack! Mop the shop!

Carlos and Meg let a duck in the shop.

Hop, hop, hop! The duck can hop on the mop.

Jack gets mad.

Do not mop the duck, Jack!

Mop the shop!

Circle all the words that end with -op.   m<u>op</u>

Why did Jack get mad?

_____

– – – – – – – – – – – – – – – – –

_____

– – – – – – – – – – – – – – – – –

_____

FIGURE 2.5 Decodable text for *-op* words.

Name:	Skill: long a review, long a w/"ing"	Words to pre-teach: says, giggle

Pancake Sunday

It's Pancake Sunday! The Pérez family is taking the subway to get pancakes. There are five of them: Mom, Dad, José, Mateo, and Maya. They're going to The Golden Pancake.

"Stay by my side," Mom says to Maya. They get off the subway. "What a gray day. Maybe the rain will hold off!"

"I see The Golden Pancake!" José starts to run, but Mateo stops him.

"No racing. Wait for the rest of us!"

Dad tells the kids to inhale. "Smell that? That's what joy smells like!"

"Who is Joy?" Maya asks.

José and Mateo giggle. "Joy smells like pancakes."

Maya shrugs. "I don't get it."

At The Golden Pancake, Dad is explaining what they want to the waitress. "And what would you like with your pancakes?" the waitress asks.

Maya says, "I want eggs. Not pancakes."

Mom and Dad are shocked. Eggs on Pancake Sunday?

But Mom smiles. "That's okay. Eggs on Pancake Sunday it is!"

Circle all of the words that end with "ing."

Why is the Pérez family taking the subway? What are they going to do?

_ _

_ _

FIGURE 2.6 Decodable text for multisyllabic words with long *a*.

confidence!) using their knowledge to read. If we present them with a text that includes lots of words that are too difficult, not only will they experience frustration but also they will spend their time using ineffective strategies (like guessing) instead of spending that time applying their knowledge.

Before you present students with a text, read it ahead of time and look for any words that students would not yet be able to decode. Plan to pre-teach those words when you introduce the text. You can do this by simply showing students these tricky words in the text and telling students what they say. If, as students are reading, you see that they have forgotten those words, you can simply tell them the word and have them continue reading.

When you introduce a decodable text to students, you can read them the title of the text and have a quick discussion about what the text will be about. There's no need to do a lengthy book walk or reveal the events or information in the text. Next, you'll want to help students make a connection between the phonics pattern(s) they've been learning and the words in the text. You can do this in a few different ways. Sometimes you might have students quickly look through the book to find a few examples of words with the target pattern. Or you might preselect two to three words from the text and present them on a whiteboard, one at a time, to have students practice decoding them with your support.

Following your book introduction, students should read the text on their own, at their own pace. If you believe that your students would benefit from a little boost to get started, you can model how or have students work as a group to decode the first sentence or two. Providing this type of support is typically only necessary when students are just beginning to read decodable texts. On the topic of beginning readers, if you're working with students who have learned their letter sounds and are just starting to read CVC words, having them read an entire decodable text might seem like too big of a jump. If you are concerned that students are not ready to tackle an entire decodable text on their own, you might try one of these two options:

- Have students read a few decodable sentences in order to build their reading muscles so that they can be successful with decodable texts. You can create your own sentences, each with one to two CVC words, plus a few simple high-frequency words that students already know. (You can also download a free set of decodable sentences for beginning readers at `fromsoundstospelling.com/book`.) When you have students read these sentences, you'll want to model and discuss skills like pointing one time under each word, saying the sounds in a word and blending, persisting after getting stuck on a word, and looking for known high-frequency words that students can read without sounding them out.

- Break up a decodable text into chunks. Students might tackle half of a book or passage on one day, and then finish the text the next day. Because beginning readers often decode slowly, this chunking strategy can make reading a decodable text more manageable.

We also want to monitor our own beliefs about our beginning readers' ability to read decodable texts on their own. As educators, we want students to feel successful, and sometimes we might hesitate to present students with a task that could be potentially frustrating to them. The reality, however, is that most students are going to find reading difficult at first! We can be selective about the types of text we ask students to read, avoiding those with phonics patterns that students haven't yet learned. We can also monitor our students to make sure that they are not becoming so frustrated that they completely shut down and lose motivation. However, we still want to challenge them! If you're not sure if students are ready to read a decodable text, why not try one out? If you find that the text is too difficult, you can always stop students and model how to finish reading it. Sometimes our students will surprise us with their abilities and persistence!

After students finish reading a decodable text, it's time for a discussion. You can have students retell the text and/or ask a few questions to evaluate their basic comprehension of the text. Discussing the meaning of the text immediately after reading helps send students the message that the purpose of reading is to understand the text. That said, be aware that students' comprehension might not be particularly strong after just one read of the text, especially if they are beginning readers or if decoding the text was challenging for them. During that first read, students are working on accurately decoding the words. This will occupy most of their working memory, so they will have less attention available to focus on making meaning from the text. Therefore, although it's valuable to discuss the meaning of the text after that first read, students' understanding of the text will likely deepen after multiple reading(s) during subsequent lesson(s).

In addition to discussing the meaning of the text, you'll want to go over any words that students found challenging to decode. You might have students turn back to a particular page of the text, locate the tricky word, and work as a group to decode it. Sometimes you might choose to write the word on a whiteboard instead so that it's removed from the context of the sentence and students cannot use other clues to figure out the word. After you help students decode the word, discuss any relevant phonics features. You might ask questions like, "What is the vowel sound in this word?" or "Which two letters work together to represent the long *o* sound, /ō/?" or "How did you know that the vowel in this word was a long vowel sound?" or "Where is the digraph in this word?" or "What is the second syllable in this word?"

Many times, you'll also want to reinforce the connection between the phonics pattern you've been teaching and the text they just read. For example, if you've been working on the *oi* pattern, you'll want students to recognize examples of the *oi* pattern in the text. Even though you've already done some of this at the beginning of the lesson, it's worth revisiting now that students have read the text. You might have students work with a partner to locate examples of words with the target pattern. Students could make a list on a whiteboard or a sticky note. If time permits, you might choose to extend the lesson with some word building or dictation related to the target skill and the text. In the next sessions, we'll explore what these activities can look like.

Word Building

Now that we've discussed a few different routines for having students decode (read) words, we'll tackle *encoding*. You might think of encoding as the opposite of decoding. In encoding activities, students take the sounds in a word and write them down in order to spell the word. Students usually *segment* (say the individual sounds of a word) before they spell the word.

Word building is one example of an effective multisensory activity that can be used to practice encoding. You might incorporate word building after you've introduced a phonics pattern and given students opportunities to read individual words with that pattern. Here's an example that might take place after the teacher has introduced the concept of silent *e* words with long *a*, and after students have read some of these words. Students use sets of magnetic letters (see Figure 2.7) to build words.

Teacher: Now that you've read some words that have long a spelled with silent *e*, let's spell some words with this pattern. Please take out your magnetic letters. (Students each take out a magnetic board with magnetic tiles for each letter.)

Teacher: Our first word is *rake*. I had to rake the leaves that covered my lawn. Say *rake*.

Students: *Rake*.

Teacher: Tell me the sounds in the word *rake*.

Students: /r/ /ā/ /k/.

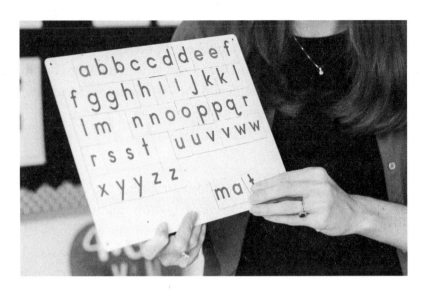

FIGURE 2.7 Building words with magnetic letter tiles.

Teacher: Good! Now build *rake* with your letters. (Students work on spelling the word rake; teacher monitors but does not yet provide corrective feedback. Students are encouraged to segment the word *rake* on their own as much as needed, as they gather the necessary letters.)

Teacher: Okay, let's say and tap the sounds in the word. As you say each sound in *rake*, you'll point under the letter or letters that represent the sound. Ready?

Students: (pointing under the r, a, and k on their own boards): /r/ /ā/ /k/, *rake*.

Teacher: If you noticed you made a mistake, go ahead and fix it now. (Pause) How do I spell *rake*?

Students: *r-a-k-e*.

Teacher: (Writes *rake* on the board so students can see it.) Check your work and fix it if you need to! (Pause) Now let's say and tap the sounds again.

Students: (pointing under the *r*, *a*, and *k* on their own boards): /r/ /ā/ /k/.

Teacher: What word is that?

Students: *Rake*!

Teacher: How did you know that you needed the silent *e* at the end?

Student(s): The *a* said its name.

Teacher: Right! When there's an *e* at the end of the word, the other vowel says its name. When you heard the /ā/ sound, you knew you needed the silent *e* to make the letter *a* say its name, /ā/. Good!

At this point, the teacher can have students clear their boards and spell an entirely different word, or they can have students change one letter in *rake* to make a new word like *take* or *rate*. Asking students to determine how to change a word by one sound helps reinforce the relationships between the sounds and letters in the words.

If you work with beginning readers or students who struggle with segmenting, you can provide more support than was described in this example. You might say, "Listen to me segment the word first" before asking students to segment it as a group. After segmenting it twice, you might also proceed sound by sound through the word. For example: "What was the first sound in *rake*?" (/r/) "Find the letter for the /r/ sound." "What was the second sound in *rake*?" (/ā/) "Find the letter or letters for the /ā/ sound." (And so on.)

Depending on how long it takes students to build words, you might have them practice building between three and eight words in each practice session. You'll want to select words carefully so that they only include patterns students have already been taught. If you have just finished teaching a specific skill (long *a* with silent *e*, in this example), you'll want to include many words with that skill. However, it's also helpful to include review words with patterns that you've also taught recently.

Additionally, it's beneficial to mix in words that are similar to—but spelled slightly differently than—the phonics pattern you're currently working on. In the long *a* with silent *e* example, the teacher might only include words that contain long *a* spelled with silent *e* that day, because students are just learning this pattern for the first time. However, a day or two later, the teacher might mix in some short *a* words (like *bat* or *glad*) to ensure that students understand the differences between short *a* and long *a* words, as well as maintain their proficiency with short *a* words. Practicing each phonics pattern in isolation is not enough; students need opportunities to compare the sounds and spellings of similar or related words (Bear et al., 2016).

Word building can be done in a whole-group or small-group setting. To make the most of your instructional time, ensure that students each have their own set of magnetic letters and that they keep them organized in alphabetical order. At the beginning of the school year, or whenever you introduce word building, take time to teach students how to keep the letters alphabetized. You might need to review this expectation throughout the year.

It's important to know that, in addition to helping students gain spelling proficiency, encoding activities like word building also improve students' reading skills. Reading and spelling are reciprocal processes, so growth in one area supports growth in the other area (Conrad et al., 2013). Therefore, even if we are very focused on getting our students to learn how to read, we don't want to skip over any encoding activities!

Wondering how to use a word-building routine with your pre-readers or students who aren't yet ready to build words on their own? One option is to have students work on spelling individual sounds. You might ask students to "find the letter that represents the /*f*/ sound," for example. After students locate and take out the letter, you ask, "What is the name of this letter?" (*f*) "What sound does it represent?" (/*f*/) This gives students an opportunity to practice their letters and gain familiarity with the organization of magnetic letters on their board.

Written Dictation

Written dictation is another effective activity for practicing encoding. In a dictation, the teacher asks students to spell specific sounds, words, and sentences, one at a time. Just like in word building, the teacher carefully selects these sounds, words, and sentences based on what students have already been taught. In addition to including words with the target phonics pattern (and any review skills), sentences might also contain high-frequency words that students have been working on.

A dictation can be done by having students write on paper or on whiteboards. In *From Sounds to Spelling*, dictations that take place earlier in the week are done on whiteboards, and a dictation at the end of the week is done on paper so that the teacher can review students' work and make instructional decisions based on this data. See Figure 2.8 for an example of a dictation completed on paper. Students were given sound boxes as a support for spelling the words. After I dictated a word and students wrote it (in the sound boxes), I then provided the correct spelling of the word for them to copy over. I followed a similar procedure for the sentence, where I dictated the sentence, had students write it, and then had them copy the sentence over correctly.

Figure 2.8 shows an example dictation of words and a sentence, but you can also dictate individual sounds for students to spell. If you'd like to dictate a few sounds for students (two to five total), it might go something like this:

Teacher: The sound is /l/. Say /l/.

Students: /l/.

Teacher: Write a letter for the sound /l/. (Students write *l*). What letter did you write?

Students: L.

Teacher: Yes! *L* can represent the /l/ sound. (Writes the letter *l* so students can see it.) Say *l*, /l/.

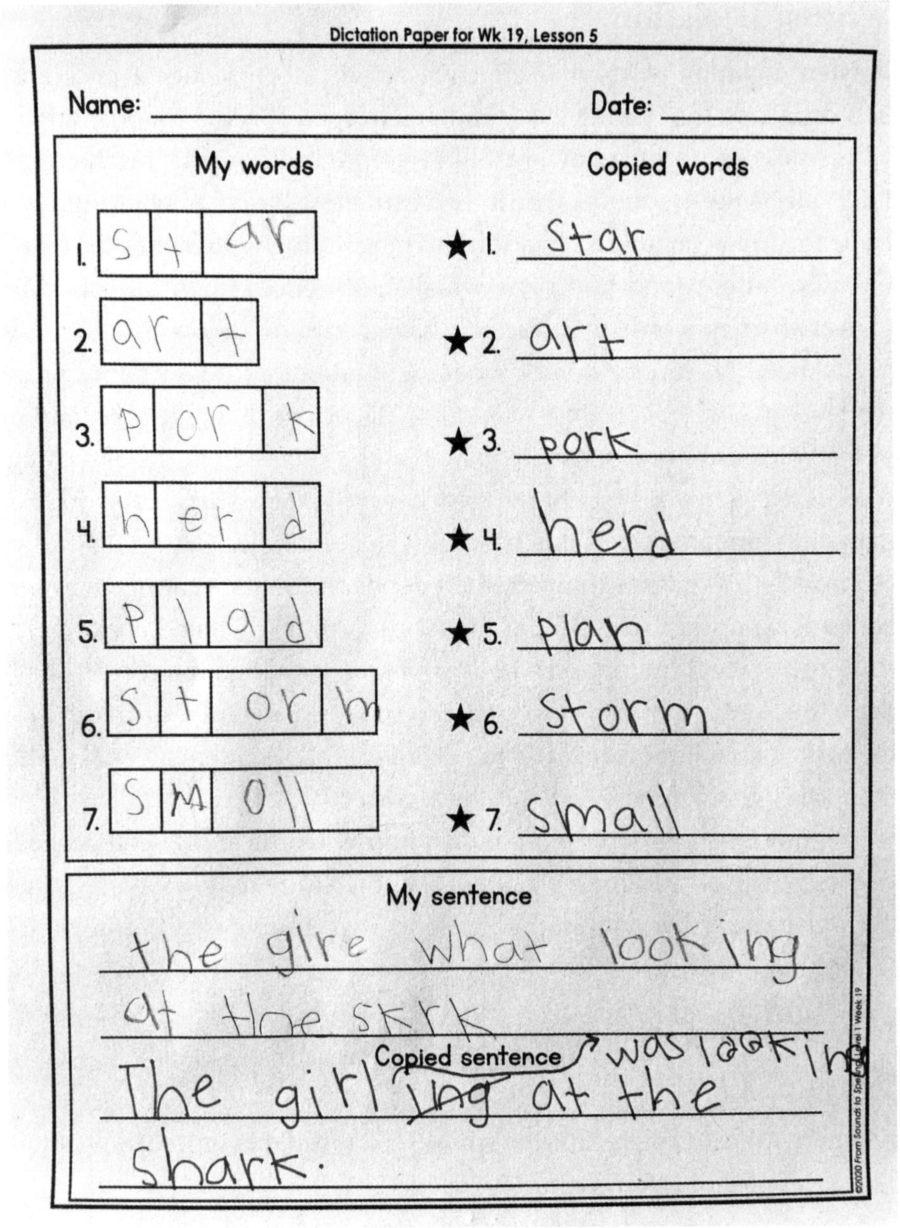
Dictation Paper for Wk 19, Lesson 5

Name: ________ Date: ________

My words	Copied words
1. s | t | ar	★ 1. Star
2. ar | t	★ 2. art
3. p | or | k	★ 3. pork
4. h | er | d	★ 4. herd
5. p | l | a | d	★ 5. plan
6. s | t | or | m	★ 6. Storm
7. s | m | o | ll	★ 7. small

My sentence

the gire what looking at the skrk

Copied sentence

The girl ~~ing~~ was looking at the shark.

©2020 From Sounds to Spelling Level 1 Week 19

FIGURE 2.8 Example dictation.

Students: *L, /l/.*

Teacher: Good. Erase.

This is a great activity for students who are learning their letters. Practicing spelling individual sounds can have a tremendous impact on students' letter knowledge. However, sound dictation need not be limited to students who are learning the alphabet. Here's another example:

Teacher: The sound is /ī/. Say /ī/.

Students: /ī/.

Teacher: You know a few different ways to spell the /ī/ sound. Write them all. (Pauses while students write.) What did you come up with? (Calls on individual students for responses.) Yes, you know four ways to spell the /ī/ sound! You know *i* with a silent *e*, like in *bike*. (Writes *ie* on the board.) You know *ie*, with no consonant in between, like in *pie*. (Writes *ie* on the board.) You also know *igh*, like in *light*. (Writes *igh* on the board.) And you also know just the letter *i*, like in *hi*. (Writes *i* on the board.) Make sure that you have all four on your whiteboard!

Next, you can have students spell a few words. The number of words will vary, depending on students' abilities and how quickly they work. You might dictate anywhere from 2 to 10 words total. When you dictate these words, you'll follow the same process described in the word building activity with *rake*. However, students will be writing each word, rather than building it with magnetic letters. I recommend having students say and tap the sounds as mentioned in the *rake* example; students will simply be touching underneath each written letter instead of underneath the magnetic letters. Make sure to have students check their work before you provide corrective feedback, and ensure that students fix their work after you have revealed how to correctly spell the word.

Last, you might choose to have students write one to two sentences. Here's an example of a sentence dictation for students who have been working on consonant blends with *l*.

Teacher: Our first sentence is, "I plan to get a clock." Say that with me.

Teacher and students: I plan to get a clock.

Teacher: Now say it again.

Students: I plan to get a clock.

At this point, students might be asked to write the sentence on their own. If needed, however, you can provide more support, like this:

Teacher: What's the first word?

Students: *I.*

Teacher: Write it! (Pause) What comes next?

Students: *Plan.*

Teacher: What are the sounds in *plan*?

Students: /p/ /l/ /ă/ /n/.

Teacher: Good. Write *plan*! (Pause.) I plan . . . What comes next?

Students: *To.*

Teacher: Write *to*.

This would continue for the remaining words in the sentence. Notice how the teacher does not ask students to segment words that they have worked on as high-frequency words (*I, to, a*). It is perfectly acceptable if students choose to sound out a word like *to* on their own, but the teacher wants to see if the students can already fluently spell these words because they have been practicing. The teacher will, however, ask students to segment all other words in the sentence (*plan, get, clock*).

The goal is for students to get to a point where they can repeat the dictated sentence a few times and then work independently to recall and write the sentence on their own. We only want to provide the amount of support that is absolutely necessary (in this case, going word by word through the sentence as students write it), and we try to remove that support as soon as possible.

Once students have written the sentence, here's what comes next:

Teacher: Read your sentence to yourself. It should say, "I plan to get a clock." Check and fix your work. (Pause) Now I'll write it, and you'll copy it over correctly. Remember not to fix your work but to write the sentence again. Okay. Our first word was *I*, and I use a capital letter for that. (Writes *I*) *I* plan. What are the sounds in *plan*?

Students: /p/ /l/ /ă/ /n/.

Teacher: How do I spell it?

Students: *p-l-a-n.*

Teacher: Good. (Writes *plan*.) I plan to . . . *To* is a word I already know how to spell, *t-o.*

This goes on until the teacher has written the complete sentence correctly and students have copied it over correctly. This is also a great opportunity for brief discussions of capitalization and ending punctuation, spaces between words, and word features (e.g., *l*-blends) that students have been working on.

At first glance, dictation might appear similar to a traditional spelling test, where students are asked to memorize a specific list of words and are tested on that list at the end of the week. However, dictation differs from a spelling test in several important ways:

- In a dictation, the teacher might ask students to spell words that they did not study previously (something that is not done on a spelling test). For example, perhaps students have been working on words with *nk*, so the teacher asks them to spell *bank*, even though this is not a word they have practiced. This enables the teacher to determine if students can apply their general word knowledge to spell a new word. Remember, this is an important skill because we cannot possibly teach students all the words in the English language; we need them to learn to apply patterns to read and spell new words!

- In a dictation, the teacher typically provides corrective feedback immediately after each word is spelled (rather than correcting students' work later, as is done during a spelling test). This makes the dictation an active learning experience for students, not just an assessment. However, if you ask students to write each word or sentence correctly, without fixing their original work, this still enables you to review student work to see how they did. If you are concerned about students trying to go back and fix their original spellings, you might direct students to put down their pencils and pick up another writing utensil (e.g., a colored pencil or pen) when it's time for you to reveal how the word is spelled and have them copy it correctly.

Just like word building, dictation is incredibly helpful in improving students' spelling and reading skills.

High-Frequency Word Instruction

In *From Sounds to Spelling*, we include high-frequency word instruction as part of our phonics lessons. High-frequency words are words that are known to appear often in beginning texts. They are words like *the* or *what*—the glue that holds together sentences. You might have a list from your school to follow, or you might use a list like Dolch or Fry. Sometimes high-frequency words are referred to as *sight words*. Technically, a sight word is a word that a reader can read instantly, by sight. Our goal is to help high-frequency words (common words) become sight words for our students so that they can quickly and easily read them in texts.

High-frequency word instruction is most effective when we help students connect new words to the phonics skills they're learning—even for irregularly spelled words (McGeown et al., 2013). If you were instructed to teach high-frequency words by having students look at them and memorize them (like I was!), this might come as a surprise to you. But it's actually good news, because having students use phonics knowledge to learn high-frequency words helps them learn words more quickly.

When we teach high-frequency words, we want to help students engage with the meaning of the word, the sounds in the word, and the spelling of the word (Blevins, 2016). Here is an example routine that incorporates all three of these practices:

1. Tell students the word that you'll be working on, and have them repeat it.

2. Give students an example sentence that includes the word. This might be a sentence spoken aloud, a sentence written on the board, or a sentence in a pocket chart. (Pocket chart sentences like the one in Figure 2.9 are great for kindergarten or early first grade, because they help reinforce the concept of a word, with one per card, and can be used later to have students practice reconstructing the sentence.)

3. Have students come up with their own original sentences with the word (orally). You might have students work with a partner, taking turns saying an original sentence. This approach gives all students an opportunity to come up with sentences, rather than just calling on a few students. If you have students work with a partner, a couple of students can still share their sentences with the entire class afterward.

FIGURE 2.9 High-frequency words in a pocket chart sentence.

4. Bring students' attention to the sounds in the word. If you had the word displayed on the board or in a pocket chart, remove it. Ask students to segment the word. For example, if you're working on the word *what*, students would say: /w//ŭ//t/. Ask students how many sounds they hear in the word (three, in this example).

5. Next, show students how the sounds in the word relate to the spelling by mapping the word into sound boxes (see Figure 2.10). You'll create one box per sound in the word, so *what* would need three boxes. In this example, *wh* would go in the first box, because these two letters are working together to represent the /w/ sound. The *a* comes next, in its own box. And the *t* comes at the end.

6. Say, "Listen to see if any of these letters surprise you." Pointing under each box as you say the corresponding sound, say /w//ŭ//t/. Students should identify that the surprising sound is the /ŭ/, spelled by the letter *a*. You might ask students what sound the letter *a* usually represents, to help them understand the difference. Summarize with a clear explanation as you refer back to the word mapped in sound boxes: "If you sound out the word *what*, the *wh* digraph represents the /w/ sound, the *a* represents the /ŭ/ sound, and the *t* represents the /t/ sound. The tricky part is the sound of the letter *a*, so we need to remember that it's going to say /ŭ/ in this word."

FIGURE 2.10 High-frequency word *what* mapped into sound boxes.

7. At this point, you might have students map the word into their own set of sound boxes, practice spelling the word by saying each letter as they tap on their outstretched arms, compare *what* to previously taught words that have the /ŭ/ sound for *a* (e.g., *was*), write the word, and/or write original sentences with the word. There is no need to incorporate all of these activities the first time you teach a new word because students will need more practice with the word in the future.

There are many effective activities you can use to teach high-frequency words; this is simply one example of a routine. When you are building your own routine, make sure to give students opportunities to work with the meaning of the word, the sounds in the word, and the spelling of the word. When selecting which words to teach each week, consider choosing words that relate to the phonics pattern you're teaching. For example, you might teach the word *what* when you're working on the digraph *wh*. However, keep in mind that you might not be able to perfectly match each word to a corresponding phonics skill. Some weeks would have too many words—think about all the *wh* words, for example! Align your high-frequency word instruction to your phonics skills as much as you can, but keep in mind that the alignment won't always be perfect.

You can download a list of common high-frequency words organized by phonics pattern, as well as descriptions of how to map over 180 common high-frequency words at this link: www.fromsoundstospelling.com/book.

Phonological Awareness Practice

Phonological awareness is the awareness of and ability to work with the sounds in words (National Reading Panel, 2000):

- Counting or being able to distinguish individual words in a sentence
- Recognizing or producing rhyming words
- Working with syllables (counting syllables, clapping syllables, blending syllables to make a word: *sun-set* → *sunset*, breaking up a word into its syllables: *magazine* → *mag-a-zine*)

- Working with onset and rime (putting together onset and rime to say a whole word: *sh-eep* → *sheep*, or breaking apart a word into its onset and rime: *cake* → *c-ake*)

- Working with phonemes, the individual sounds in words (identifying the first, last, or middle sound in a word; blending sounds into words: /*ch*/ /*ā*/ /*s*/ → *chase*; segmenting words into sounds: *heart* → /*h*/ /*ar*/ /*t*/; manipulating phonemes by removing, adding, or substituting sounds: "Say *bus* without the /*b*/" → *us*)

Pure phonological awareness activities do not involve any letters or words. Skills are typically practiced through listening and speaking. Although phonological awareness is technically a separate skill set from phonics, it makes sense to incorporate phonological awareness practice into your phonics lessons. The purpose of learning phonological awareness skills is so that children can read and spell words (which you practice during your phonics lessons). Additionally, phonological awareness should, at times, be practiced alongside phonics. This is especially true after children know some sound-spelling relationships (Clemens et al., 2021).

Phonological awareness activities can be brief, lasting just a few minutes per day in kindergarten and first grade (National Reading Panel, 2000). Second graders also benefit from phonemic awareness practice, especially at the beginning of the school year, as do struggling readers. When teaching these skills in a whole-group setting, it's easiest to break up practice time into three- to five-minute chunks throughout the day (they make for great transition activities). However, if only some of your students are working on phonological awareness skills (e.g., your below-level third-grade readers), you can include these activities in their small-group instruction instead of working on them with the entire class.

Here are three examples of oral phonological awareness drills (excerpted *From Sounds to Spelling*). No letters or words are used here, and note that these examples address different skills and would not be used in the same practice session:

Example 1

Teacher: I'm going to say two words. You'll repeat the words, then show me thumbs-up if they rhyme, and thumbs-down if they don't. The words are *rash, splash*. Say the words.

Students: *Rash, splash.*

Teacher: Do they rhyme? Show me thumbs-up or thumbs-down.

Students: Thumbs-up.

Example 2

Teacher: I'm going to say the sounds in a mystery word! You repeat the sounds, then tell me what the word is. /t/ /ā/ /k/.

Students: /t/ /ā/ /k/, *take*!

Example 3

Teacher: I'll say a word, and you repeat it. Then, we'll switch out the first sound to make a different word. Ready? The word is *sip*. Say *sip*.

Students: *Sip.*

Teacher: *Sip*, change /s/ to /r/ and we get. . .

Students: *Rip*!

It can also be helpful to incorporate physical manipulatives into your phonological awareness activities. Elkonin or sound boxes (Elkonin, 1973), for example, are a great tool to help students practice phoneme segmenting. As students (or you) say each sound in a word, students slide a counter into each box (see Figure 2.11). For example, when segmenting the word *fast*, they would say, /f/ (slide one counter into the first box) /ă/ (slide a second counter into the second box), /s/ (slide a third counter into the third box), /t/ (slide a fourth counter into the fourth box). You might recognize the sound boxes from the "High-Frequency Word Instruction" section; the main difference is that here,

FIGURE 2.11 Segmenting a word into sound boxes.

for practicing the phonemic awareness skill of segmenting, you are not writing any letters into the boxes.

Picture sorts (see Figure 2.12) are another great tool for practicing phonological awareness. Students might sort pictures by one of the following attributes:

- Number of syllables

- First sound

- Last sound

- Middle vowel sound

- Number of phonemes

When you're having students sort pictures, make sure that they say the name of the picture aloud before sorting it. They will also need to say aloud the target attribute. For example, if they are sorting pictures by number of syllables, they should say each syllable aloud, as well as the number of syllables. If they are sorting pictures by middle vowel sound, they say that vowel sound (after saying the name of the picture).

Warm-Up Routines

In the activities we've covered so far, we've briefly discussed how you might incorporate review of previously taught patterns (e.g., by adding certain sounds into the blending drill, dictating words with review patterns, and so on). However, a quick warm-up routine at the start of your lesson is another way to consistently build in time to review skills.

FIGURE 2.12 Sorting pictures by first sound.

An effective warm-up routine moves quickly from one activity to the next, lasting no more than three to six minutes. You might incorporate some of the following:

- Flashcards to practice letter names, letter sounds and/or phonics patterns (e.g., *oa* or *igh*), and/or high-frequency words
- Blending drill, with previously taught sounds
- A quick phonological awareness exercise
- Songs or chants to review letters, sounds, and patterns
- A brief review game (something displayed on an interactive whiteboard, for example)

Your warm-up routine might vary somewhat from day-to-day. Regardless of what it looks like, keep the pace quick to keep students engaged, and this will help you build momentum that continues into the main portion of your lesson. A warm-up routine should also be easy for you to prepare so that you can implement it consistently.

Creating a Schedule

It's important to note that you likely will not be able to (or need to) implement all these routines on a daily basis. In the chapters that follow, you'll find example schedules that provide guidance in how often to use each routine, a suggested order of activities, and more. You'll also learn which routines you might try in a whole-group setting and which routines you can consider incorporating into your small-group instruction.

What's Next?

Now that we've covered some effective phonics routines, we'll move on to discussing how these routines fit into the three models for differentiation. Remember, it's best to approach the next three chapters with an open mind. You might find that you want to use elements from multiple models, or even use different models at different points in the school year. I also recommend reading through each example classroom scenario in the coming chapters, even if it describes a grade level different from the one you teach.

References

Baker, S. K., Santiago, R. T., Masser, J., Nelson, N. J., & Turtura, J. (2018). *The alphabetic principle: From phonological awareness to reading words*. U.S. Department of Education, Office of Elementary and Secondary Education, Office of Special Education Programs, National Center on Improving Literacy.

Bear, D. R., Invernizzi, M., Johnston, F. A., & Templeton, S. (2016). *Words their way: Word study for phonics, vocabulary, and spelling instruction*. Pearson.

Blevins, W. (2016). *A fresh look at phonics, grades K–2: Common causes of failure and 7 ingredients for success*. Corwin Press.

Clemens, N., Solari, E., Kearns, D. M., Fien, H., Nelson, N. J., Stelega, M., . . . Hoeft, F. (2021, December 14). They say you can do phonemic awareness instruction "in the dark," but should you? A critical evaluation of the trend toward advanced phonemic awareness training. https://doi.org/10.31234/osf.io/ajxbv

Conrad, N. J., Harris, N., & Williams, J. (2013). Individual differences in children's literacy development: The contribution of orthographic knowledge. *Reading and Writing, 26*, 1223–1239. https://doi.org/10.1007/s11145-012-9415-2

Elkonin, D. B. (1973). U.S.S.R. In J. Downing (Ed.). *Comparative reading: Cross-national studies of behavior and processes in reading and writing*. Macmillan.

Mattson, M. P. (2014). Superior pattern processing is the essence of the evolved human brain. *Frontiers in Neuroscience, 8*, 265. https://doi.org/10.3389/fnins.2014.00265

McGeown, S., Medford, E., & Moxon, G. (2013). Individual differences in children's reading and spelling strategies and the skills supporting strategy use. *Learning and Individual Differences, 28*, 75–81.

National Reading Panel. (2000). *Report of the National Reading Panel—teaching children to read: An Evidence-based assessment of the scientific research. Literature on reading and its implications for reading instruction*. National Institute of Child Health and Human Development. https://www.nichd.nih.gov/sites/default/files/publications/pubs/nrp/documents/report.pdf

Vaughn, S., & Fletcher, J. (2021). Explicit instruction as the essential tool for executing the science of reading. *The Reading League Journal, 2*(2), 4–11.

Model 1
Whole-Class Instruction with Built-In Differentiation

In the first model for differentiation, all students are taught the same phonics lesson, at the same time, on a daily basis. For example, the new skill introduction routine described in Chapter 2 would be done with the entire class gathered together, and it would be followed by additional practice activities. However, even though this model primarily leverages whole-group instruction, certain components of the lesson include differentiation to meet a range of student needs.

Let's take a peek at what this might look like in two scenarios: a first-grade classroom and a third-grade classroom.

Discussion of Ms. Tate's First-Grade Classroom

In Ms. Tate's first lesson on magic *e* (long *a* words spelled with silent *e*), the level of differentiation is relatively minimal. All students are learning the same content, even though some students in her class already have some level of proficiency with reading silent *e* words. Still, Ms. Tate did all of the following in order to meet a range of needs in her classroom:

- She strategically assigned partners for the magic *e* puppet activity. Students who were a bit less advanced in their phonics knowledge were paired with students who were more advanced (but not

CASE STUDY

Ms. Tate's First-Grade Classroom

Ms. Tate begins her phonics lesson with all students sitting on the rug. After a few warm-up phonological awareness activities and a review of high-frequency words on flashcards, she says, "Today we're going to learn about a special job for the letter *Ee*." She points to the letter on the classroom alphabet chart. "Let's watch a video to learn about magic *e*."

She presses play on a brief video that explains, through a story with fairytale characters, how the silent *e* at the end of a word "makes the other vowel say its name." After the video has finished, she asks students to turn to a partner and discuss what they've just learned.

"Now that you know the story of magic *e*," says Ms. Tate, "Let's practice reading some magic *e* words with the vowel *a*." She directs students to spread out around the classroom and sit with their assigned partner. Ms. Tate hands each pair of children a list of short *a* words and a magic *e* puppet that has the letter *e* on a craft stick. Ms. Tate models how to read the first short *a* word on the list (*mad*), then how to place the magic *e* puppet at the end to make the word *made* and read the new, long vowel word, *made* (see Figure 3.1). Students work with their partners to read the rest of the words, first with short vowels, then with long vowels.

Last, Ms. Tate asks students to take out their magnetic letters. Each child has their own set. Some students also take out a laminated strip of sound boxes, a tool that helps them with segmenting (see Figure 3.2). Ms. Tate says,

"We're going to build the word *tap*. I might tap someone on the shoulder to get them to look at me. Say *tap*." The students repeat the word. "Now build it!" Some students build the word quickly and easily, as they have a high level of proficiency with CVC (consonant-vowel-consonant) words. Other students use their strip of sound boxes to segment the word (/t/ /ă/ /p/), touching a box as they say each sound, and then they build the word. Ms. Tate helps one child with this task. After Ms. Tate shows students how to spell the word correctly so they can check their work, she says, "Now let's take *tap* and change it into the word *tape*. Turn and tell the person sitting next to you how you're going to do this." Students briefly discuss, and the class comes to the consensus that this can be accomplished by adding the letter *e* at the end. Once students have finished building *tape*, Ms. Tate says, "Great job! Now let's say each sound in the word and tap under it. Remember that the silent *e* at the end won't make a sound!" Students tap under each letter, saying "/t/ /ā/ /p/, *tape*." Ms. Tate asks them to clear their magnetic boards. She repeats this procedure for two more words, *cap/cape* and *man/mane*. At this point, the allotted time for the phonics lesson is over. Ms. Tate asks students to tell their partner what they learned about silent *e* at the end of the word, and then the class transitions to their work in another subject area.

In the days to come, students continue practicing long *a* words spelled with silent *e*.

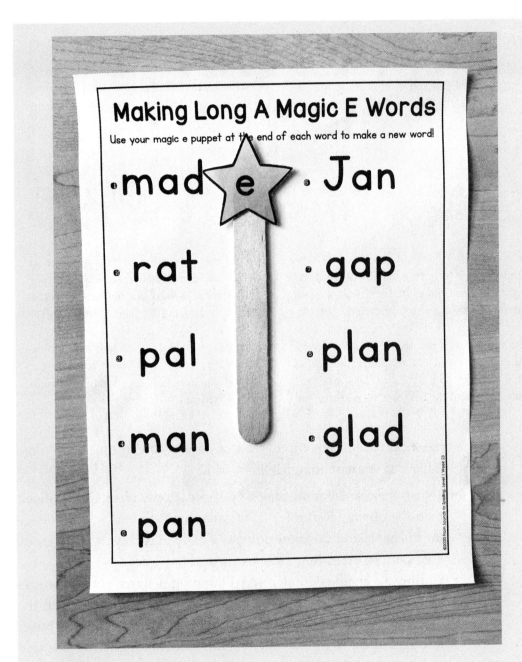

FIGURE 3.1 Making long *a* words with a magic *e* puppet.

FIGURE 3.2 Sound boxes for segmenting.

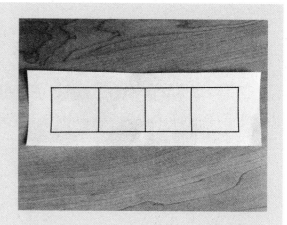

In one activity, they read lists of words. Some students receive a list with CVC *e* words like *made* and *game*. Other students, who are more advanced, read a list that includes CCVC *e* words like *skate* and *brave*. The more advanced list also includes plurals like *grapes* and *plates*. Additionally, students practice reading decodable passages with long *a* words spelled with silent *e*. Ms. Tate has two versions of each passage, one more difficult than the other so that she can appropriately challenge different students in her class. When students are asked to spell words using magnetic letters or dry-erase boards, Ms. Tate includes different types of long a silent e words. She knows that certain words (e.g., *shapes* or *grate*) will be tricky for certain students but an appropriate challenge for other students.

drastically more advanced, as a large gap can result in the more advanced student doing all the work).

- Two of the words for the magic *e* puppet activity were more difficult than the others (*glad*, *plan*). This gave some students the challenge they needed, and the more advanced child in each pair could guide their partner in reading these two words.
- During the magnetic letter word-building activity, some students took out their segmenting strips in order to help them spell the CVC words. All students practice segmenting and use sound boxes throughout the year, but only certain students needed to use segmenting strips for this particular activity. This simple tool provided them with the extra support they needed to be successful with spelling the CVC words.

When you use the whole-class model and are first introducing a skill, such as in this example lesson, the amount of differentiation you can provide might be limited. This is perfectly fine. Follow-up lessons on the skill provide more opportunities for differentiation. For example, in Ms. Tate's class, a word reading activity on the following day was easily differentiated with two separate word lists for students to practice. Spelling activities also incorporated a range of words, some with digraphs, blends, and the plural -s ending that were designed for students who needed a challenge. All students in the class practice spelling all these words, even the more challenging ones, so Ms. Tate steps in to provide extra help to students who need it.

In addition to her core phonics lesson, Ms. Tate has time set aside in her literacy block for skills-based small-group instruction. These small groups address a variety of reading skills, including phonics. Some groups need extra practice with previously taught phonics skills, and some groups are ready for more advanced phonics skills. Small groups provide an opportunity to supplement her phonics lessons, even though core instruction takes place in a whole-group setting.

Now that we've seen a first-grade example of differentiation as part of whole-group phonics instruction, let's take a look at a third-grade example.

Discussion of Mr. Suarez's Third-Grade Classroom

In Mr. Suarez's initial lesson on the *sion* syllable, all students receive the same core introduction to the skill. Students practice the skill with the *tion/sion* sort. Mr. Suarez can easily differentiate the sort by providing different groups of students with different words. Although he doesn't sit down and teach an entire small-group lesson, he still checks in with each group to make sure that they can decode the words and understand what the words mean.

CASE STUDY

Mr. Suarez's Third-Grade Classroom

Mr. Suarez writes -*tion* on the board so all students can see it. "Okay, class," he says. "Do you remember what *tion* sounds like in a word?"

Students reply, "/*shŭn*/ or /*shĭn*/."

"Correct," Mr. Suarez says, and he writes the word *action* on the board. "So this word would say . . ."

Students reply, "*Action*."

Mr. Suarez then writes -*sion* on the board. "Today we're going to learn about another way to spell /shŭn/ or /shĭn/, with the syllable *s-i-o-n*. Just like *t-i-o-n*, *s-i-o-n* is an unstressed syllable that appears at the end of a word. It has a *schwa* for the vowel sound, /ŭ/ or /ĭ/."

He writes the word *man* on the board and asks students to read it. Then, he adds the letters *sion* at the end and says, "If the first syllable here is *man*, what does this word say?"

Students reply, "*Mansion*."

"Right! A mansion is a very big house. In this word, *s-i-o-n* sounded like /*shŭn*/ or /*shĭn*/, depending on how you pronounce it. But *s-i-o-n* can also sound like /*zhŭn*/ or /*zhĭn*/. Let me give you an example."

Mr. Suarez writes the word *vision* on the board. "The first part will say /*vĭ*/. The second part will say /*zhĭn*/, spelled by *s-i-o-n*. What word is this?"

Students reply, "*Vision*."

Mr. Suarez says, "Yes! When you go to the optometrist, or the eye doctor, they check your vision to find out how well you can see. In *mansion*, what did *s-i-o-n* sound like?"

Students reply, "/*shĭn*/."

"Yes," says Mr. Suarez. "And in *vision*, what did *s-i-o-n* sound like?"

Students reply, "/*zhĭn*/."

"Exactly," Mr. Suarez responds. "That *s-i-o-n* ending can represent /*shĭn*/ or /*zhĭn*/, and even sound like /*shŭn*/ or /*zhŭn*/. It's a tricky one!"

Next, Mr. Suarez has students read the words *session* and *evasion*. The class discusses what each word means. Then, he divides the kids into three groups. Students move to sit with their groupmates at tables, and Mr. Suarez passes out word sorts. Each child receives a sorting mat and words to sort, but each group's words are different (see Figure 3.3). Group 1's words include two-syllable *tion* and *sion* words, and they are given fewer total words than the other groups. Group 2's words include two- and three-syllable *tion* and *sion* words. Group 3's words include two-, three-, and four- syllable *tion* and *sion* words.

Mr. Suarez asks each group to work together to read their words. While students are going through the process of reading the words and then cutting the word cards apart, he spends a few minutes touching base with each group. During those few minutes, he ensures that students can decode the words accurately, and he also explains the meaning of words that are less familiar to students.

Last, students work independently to sort their words, reading each word once again. Students are allowed to ask each other for help with reading the words, if needed. Mr. Suarez continues visiting each group to make sure that

Group 1

action	fusion	ration
mission	caption	lotion
option	vision	motion
nation	fission	tension

Group 2

fusion	tension	revision
audition	eviction	options
occasion	rations	friction
fission	mission	motion
lesion	infusion	devotion
ambition	nation	caption

Group 3

fusion	apprehension	revision
audition	eviction	fascination
occasion	rations	friction
fission	mission	intermission
lesion	infusion	devotion
ambition	exposition	caption

FIGURE 3.3 Differentiated word sort for *-tion/-sion*.

they are on the right track. Students do not glue down their word cards because they will practice sorting the words again, later in the week.

In subsequent lessons, Mr. Suarez continues to differentiate as students practice multisyllabic words. When students read decodable passages with *sion* words, for example, some students read only half of the passage per day,

and others read the entire passage in one sitting. On one occasion, Mr. Suarez meets with each group to have them practice spelling words with *tion* and *sion*. He has already had the class spell two-syllable words with these ending syllables, but he wants to provide further practice with groups 1 and 2 and give group 3 a chance to practice spelling three-syllable words.

During the rest of the week, Mr. Suarez differentiates by varying the amount of text that students are asked to read, and by varying the length and difficulty of the words that students are asked to spell. He monitors student progress and makes changes to his groups and activities based on what he notices.

In addition to these examples of differentiation, Mr. Suarez also discusses phonics and word patterns with students during some of his small-group reading lessons. This word work is quick and supplementary, because most of it takes place during his dedicated time for whole-group phonics lessons. Still, adding a bit of word work to his small groups enables him to focus on skills that are the most relevant to each group of students.

Leveraging Leveled Materials

In both examples, the teachers use different leveled materials with different students. All students are working on the same core skill (long *a* words spelled with silent *e*, or words with *sion*), but sometimes different students read and spell different words with those skills. The length and difficulty of texts that students are asked to read also differ. Using or creating different-leveled materials is a great way to differentiate, especially when most of your phonics instruction takes place in a whole-group setting. You can hand different groups of students different tasks to work on, even if you're not able to teach complete small-group lessons.

You might wonder, "Won't students notice that they are getting different work from other students?" And the answer is, most likely, yes. Students naturally notice differences between themselves and others. Most children have a strong preference for everyone getting the same thing, because their brains deem this to be "fair." Interestingly, this sense of fairness appears to be innate. In one study (Sloane et al., 2012), 19- to 21-month-old babies watched two scenarios. Researchers observed the babies and noted the lengths of their stares, because babies stare longer when something surprises them or goes against their expectations. In both scenarios, the babies stared longer when they observed something inequitable (one giraffe puppet receiving more toys than another puppet, and two women receiving rewards for cleaning up when only one did the work). This indicates that, even from a very young age, children begin to expect that people should all be treated the same way.

As adults, we know that fair does not necessarily mean precisely equal. For example, it is not unfair that some children wear glasses so that they can see the board in class, even though the other students do not wear glasses. We also know that it would be *more* unfair to always give all students the same exact same work to complete, if we know that we could better meet their needs by providing differentiated work. It's our job, therefore, to help students develop a more robust understanding of what is fair.

When we differentiate our phonics instruction (or any content, for that matter), we need to have conversations with our students, many times throughout the year, to help them understand that it's okay for different kids to complete different types of work. Be proactive in helping students manage their feelings about a perceived lack of fairness. Before you begin differentiated activities, have a discussion with students to explain that all kids (and human beings) need different things. Try giving an example like a step stool, something that certain people use to reach the sink, whereas others do not need it. You might also come up with a line you say repeatedly, like, "We all have different work, and that's okay!" You might eventually hear students repeating that same line to themselves or to each other. An excellent book to read aloud is Courtney Butorac's *That's Not Fair! A Book About How Fair Is Not Always Equal*.

Types of Leveled Materials

Let's take a closer look at some different kinds of leveled materials that you might use with your students. All materials pictured here come from the phonics program *From Sounds to Spelling*, but the overall concepts can be used within any program.

Word Lists for Blending

After teaching students a phonics skill, you'll want to have them practice applying that knowledge to word reading, as we discussed in Chapter 2. Leveled word lists are an easy differentiation tool that you can incorporate into your instruction. Students can all read word lists at the same time, but different groups of students might work with different lists (see Figure 3.4 for an on-level list of words with *r*-controlled *a*, and Figure 3.5 for a below-level list on the same skill).

If you decide to create your own word lists, you might start with your core list that includes words appropriate for an average student in the class. You can then create an easier list, as well as a more difficult list, by using one or several of the strategies featured in Table 3.1. A range of options are included in Table 3.1, but they will not all be relevant to students in grades K–3.

If you are short on time or want to avoid creating multiple word lists, another option is to create a two-column word list. When you pass out

AR Words Practice
Wk 19 Lvl 1

art	park	shark
arm	star	start
far	harm	Review
part	hard	spilled
car	scar	checking

©2020 From Sounds to Spelling, Level 1 Week 19

FIGURE 3.4 On-level list of AR words.

AR Words Practice (E)
Wk 19 Lvl 1

art	park
arm	star
far	hard
part	shark
car	start

FIGURE 3.5 Below-level list of AR words.

Table 3.1 Strategies for Making a Word List Easier or More Difficult

To Make a List Easier	To Make a List More Difficult
• Include fewer words. • Use only base words, no plurals or endings (e.g., *hat, seat, shout*). • Omit words with digraphs or blends (if applicable). • Stick with one-syllable words (e.g., *cake, deep*).	• Include more words (as long as you are intentional about the words you select; avoid lengthening lists for the sole purpose of creating busywork). • Use words with inflectional endings -*s*, -*ed*, and/or -*ing* (e.g., *hats, seated, shouting*). • Add words with digraphs or blends (e.g., *chase, street*). • Incorporate words with two or more syllables (e.g., *cupcake, deepen*).

the list, tell students to fold their papers in half. Instruct them to read the first column, and tell them that the second column (which has been folded back) is a bonus challenge. Your more advanced students will finish the first column and move on to the more challenging words, and your less advanced students will likely spend the allotted time working on the first column.

If you use the strategy of differentiated word lists, assess students regularly to ensure that you are continuing to give them words appropriate for their level. It only takes a moment to listen to a child read a word list while the other students are working on their own lists. It's also important to give lower-performing students an opportunity to try out harder words, too. Sometimes your students might surprise you!

Word Sorts

As we discussed in Chapter 2, word sorts are an excellent tool that help students attend to patterns in words and compare similar words. Just like Mr. Suarez did, you can provide different groups of students with different lists of words to sort (refer to Figure 3.3). Later, you can ask students to practice spelling the words that they sorted.

To differentiate your word sorts while still having all students work on the same core skill, you can use the strategies described in the previous section on creating differentiated word lists (e.g., using or omitting words with inflectional endings, varying the number of syllables, etc.). Make sure to spend a little time with each group of students so you can provide support with decoding the words, as well as input on the meanings of the words. We don't want students simply sorting words without being able to decode them or understand what the words mean!

Decodable Texts

In addition to having students read individual words with a target phonics skill, you'll also want to have them practice reading entire texts for that skill (decodable texts). Often, decodable texts are written at only one difficulty level. For example, a reading program provides just one text on *ch* for all students to read. This, however, is unfortunate, because even though all students might be working on the same skill, they might differ in areas like high-frequency word knowledge and reading fluency. Some students, for example, take longer to decode words than others, so they need shorter texts to read. Some of your students might be language learners who benefit from simpler sentence structure. For this reason, in *From Sounds to Spelling*, we included two different difficulty levels for many of the decodable texts. This enables teachers to select the text that's the most appropriate for their students' needs.

If you don't have access to decodable texts at multiple difficulty levels, you might occasionally choose to create different versions of a short decodable passage for students to read. Start with a pre-written passage, then create versions that are easier and/or more difficult, depending on the needs of your students. See Table 3.2 for some strategies to guide you.

Just like with the word lists and word sorts, it's important to assess students so you aren't incorrectly giving them a text that is much too easy or too difficult. In each text, you'll want there to be challenges for students to work through, as well as words and sentences that are easier for them. Something else to remember is that the support *you* provide can help make a text easier or more difficult. You might be able to use the same decodable text with all students, but perhaps most of your students read it independently, and some of your students meet with you in a small group. In that small group, you might break up the text over two days, have students practice decoding a few of the words prior to reading the text, pre-teach a high-frequency word that students don't know yet, and/or chorally read the first sentence or two of the text as a group. Texts at different levels are great, but you can still make

Table 3.2 Strategies for Making a Decodable Text Easier or More Difficult

To Make a Text Easier	To Make a Text More Difficult
• Make it shorter. • Include easier words (see the suggestions in the "Word Lists for Blending" section). • Use shorter sentences.	• Make it longer (within reason). • Include more challenging words (see the suggestions in the "Word Lists for Blending" section). • Add more clauses, adjectives, and/or adverbs to sentences.

single-level texts work when you vary the amount of support that you provide students.

Finally, always remember to follow copyright law when creating your own versions of texts. (Typically, writing your own adaptations is permitted as long as they are only used in the classroom, with your students, but always refer to your local copyright laws.)

Final Thoughts on Leveled Materials

These tools are just a starting point, and sometimes you won't need printed, physical materials in order to differentiate. For example, when you ask students to build or write words, include a few easier/review words in your list, as well as a challenge word or two. When you work with an entire class of students, it's simply not possible to ensure that each and every task provides the "perfect" level of challenge for every single student. The best we can do is include a variety of difficulty levels, and provide extra support to students who need it.

Putting It All Together: Example Schedules

Now that you have some information about whole-class instruction with built-in differentiation, you might be wondering, "What does this look like on a daily and weekly basis?" In this section, we'll explore some example schedules for late kindergarten and first grade, second grade, and third grade. A schedule for early kindergarten is included in Chapter 7 with the discussion of alphabet instruction. These K–3 schedules include approximately 30 minutes' worth of activities, and the third grade schedule includes about 20 minutes' worth of activities (see Tables 3.3, 3.4, and 3.5). Remember that the schedules are simply a starting point; you might have more or less time allotted for instruction, and you might need to do more or less differentiation, depending on your students' needs.

Table 3.3 Late Kindergarten or First-Grade Sample Schedule with Differentiation Model 1

Monday	Tuesday	Wednesday	Thursday	Friday
• Phonological awareness warm-up (2–3 minutes) • Review activities: sounds on flashcards, high-frequency word flashcards (3 minutes) • Introduce new concept/skill (3–5 minutes) • Multisensory writing with new skill and review (3 minutes) • Blending drill with new skill (3–4 minutes) • Word building with new skill (5 minutes)	• Phonological awareness warm-up (2–3 minutes) • Review activities: sounds on flashcards, high-frequency word flashcards, blending drill (4 minutes) • Introduce new high-frequency word(s) (5 minutes) • Read words with Monday's new skill (4–5 minutes) • Spell words on whiteboards with Monday's new skill (4–5 minutes) • Read decodable text with Monday's new skill (4–10 minutes)	• Phonological awareness warm-up (2–3 minutes) • Review activities: sounds on flashcards, high-frequency word flashcards (3 minutes) • Introduce new concept/skill (3–5 minutes) • Multisensory writing with new skill and review (3 minutes) • Blending drill with new skill (2–3 minutes) • Word building with new skill (4 minutes) • Introduce word sort to compare Monday's skill with today's new skill (2- to 3-minute introduction; students can work on the sort immediately or later on)	• Phonological awareness warm-up (2–3 minutes) • Review activities: sounds on flashcards, high-frequency word flashcards, blending drill (4 minutes) • Optional: handwriting practice (3–10 minutes) • Word reading with Wednesday's new skill (2–3 minutes) • Sort and write (5–7 minutes) • Optional; for first grade only: practice dividing and reading multisyllabic words with this week's new skills (5 minutes) • Read decodable text with Wednesday's new skill (4–10 minutes)	• Phonological awareness warm-up (2–3 minutes) • Review activities: sounds on flashcards, high-frequency word flashcards, blending drill (3–4 minutes) • Dictation (10 minutes) • Reread decodable texts from this week and play games (10+ minutes)

Table 3.4 Second-Grade Sample Schedule with Differentiation Model 1

Monday	Tuesday	Wednesday	Thursday	Friday
• Review activities: sounds/patterns, high-frequency words (2–3 minutes)	• Review activities: sounds/patterns, high-frequency words (2–3 minutes)	• Review activities: sounds/patterns, high-frequency words (2–3 minutes)	• Review activities: sounds/patterns, high-frequency words (2–3 minutes)	• Review activities: sounds/patterns, high-frequency words (2–3 minutes)
• Optional: phonological awareness warm-up (2–3 minutes)	• Optional: phonological awareness (2–3 minutes)	• Optional: phonological awareness warm-up (2–3 minutes)	• Optional: phonological awareness warm-up (2–3 minutes)	• Optional: phonological awareness warm-up (2–3 minutes)
• Introduce new skill (2–4 minutes)	• Introduce new high-frequency word(s) (5 minutes)	• Introduce new skill (2–4 minutes)	• Optional: handwriting practice (3–10 minutes)	• Dictation (10 minutes)
• Read words with the new skill (2–4 minutes)	• Review Monday's new skill; read one-syllable and multisyllabic words with the new skill (5 minutes)	• Read words with the new skill (2–4 minutes)	• Sort and write with Monday's and Wednesday's new skills (6–8 minutes)	• Reread decodable texts from this week and play games (10+ minutes)
• Multisensory writing with new skill + review (3 minutes)	• Whiteboard dictation (5–6 minutes)	• Multisensory writing with new skill and review (3 minutes)	• Practice breaking up and decoding multisyllabic words (5–7 minutes)	
• Word building with new skill (4–5 minutes)	• Read decodable text with Monday's new skill (5–10 minutes)	• Word building with new skill (5 minutes)	• Read decodable text with Wednesday's new skill (5–10 minutes)	
		• Introduce word sort to compare Monday's skill with today's new skill (2- to 3-minute introduction; students can work on the sort immediately or later on)		

Table 3.5 Third-Grade Sample Schedule with Differentiation Model 1

Monday	Tuesday	Wednesday	Thursday	Friday
• Review activities: sounds/patterns, high-frequency words (2–3 minutes) • Introduce new skill; optional multisensory writing with new skill (3–5 minutes) • Read one-syllable and/or multisyllabic words with the new skill (3–4 minutes) • Word building with new skill (4–5 minutes)	• Review activities: sounds/patterns, high-frequency words (2–3 minutes) • Review Monday's new skill; read one-syllable and/or multisyllabic words with the new skill (4 minutes) • Whiteboard dictation (4–5 minutes) • Read decodable text with Monday's new skill (5–8 minutes)	• Review activities: sounds/patterns, high-frequency words (2–3 minutes) • Introduce new skill; optional multisensory writing with new skill (3–5 minutes) • Read one-syllable and/or multisyllabic words with the new skill (3–4 minutes) • Word building with new skill (4–5 minutes) • Introduce word sort to compare Monday's skill with today's new skill (2- to 3-minute introduction; students can work on the sort immediately or later on)	• Review activities: sounds/patterns, high-frequency words (2–3 minutes) • Review Wednesday's new skill; read one-syllable and/or multisyllabic words with the new skill (4 minutes) • Sort and write with Monday's and Wednesday's new skills (6–8 minutes) • Read decodable text with Wednesday's new skill (5–8 minutes)	• Review activities: sounds/patterns, high-frequency words (2–3 minutes) • Dictation (10 minutes) • Reread decodable texts from this week and play games (7+ minutes)

Organizing Your Physical Space

When you decide how to organize your classroom and materials to implement this model for differentiation, ask yourself, "How can I set up the space in order to maximize instructional time?" This guiding question can make many of your decisions easier.

When you're introducing a new concept, it's often easiest to have students sit on a rug in front of you in order to help minimize distractions that might be present when they're sitting at their desks or tables (e.g., the temptation to play with materials inside their desks). You'll typically want to create a teaching station that includes a chair, small table, access to a whiteboard or interactive board, writing utensils, your own set of magnetic letters or tiles, and preferably a document camera so that you can create an enlarged display of any materials you're working with. Keep any resources you'll need for each lesson (e.g., flashcards, handouts) nearby. You might choose to set up drawers or bins organized by each day of the week so that you can quickly and easily locate what you need.

It's also important to consider how you organize students' materials. First, list out the materials that students will need on a regular basis (e.g., sets of magnetic letters and boards, whiteboards, markers, whiteboard erasers, pencils, a certain type of writing paper). All materials should be easily accessible to students so that they can be quickly obtained during a lesson in order to maximize instructional time. For example, instead of you or a student volunteer passing out whiteboards to students, place a bin at each table that contains whiteboards, markers, and erasers. You can choose a table leader to pass out materials to all students at their table. This strategy saves time even if students are not sitting with their table group to do the activity (e.g., they are sitting on the rug). You might also choose to create phonics folders for students where they store materials they'll need to access for more than one day (e.g., decodable texts to reread). Phonics folders can also be used as a tool for differentiation, because you can place different materials in different students' folders ahead of a lesson (e.g., different versions of a word list or word sort).

Students will need to be explicitly taught how to access and use materials appropriately. This is best done at the beginning of the school year but will also likely need to be reviewed later. For example, if students are expected to keep their magnetic letters in alphabetical order, model how to do this, and give them multiple opportunities to practice alphabetizing. If students will be using whiteboard markers, talk about attaching the cap to the end of the marker so that they don't lose it while they are writing. Discuss safety expectations, particularly for materials like scissors. When teaching students about each material at the beginning of the year, you can also let students freely explore it for a few minutes before they are expected to use the material for academic purposes.

Strengths and Limitations of This Model

Similar to any instructional choice you make, this model (whole-class instruction with built-in differentiation) comes with its advantages and disadvantages. One advantage of this model is that, when compared to the other two models, it typically provides students with the most instructional time for phonics each day. It's important for students to receive phonics instruction on a daily basis, and it's often easier to make this happen when you have time set aside for whole-class lessons.

Another advantage of this model is that it can be easier on teachers in terms of planning and preparing materials. In this model, students are all doing the same routines and activities, which cuts down on the number of materials teachers need to create or prepare. Although some materials might be leveled (e.g., word lists), you can create or locate these resources once and use them year after year. With all of the expectations placed on teachers and only limited time in the workday, these time savings are important.

Of course, this model comes with its disadvantages, too. When you're teaching phonics in a whole-class setting, differentiation is inherently more difficult. You're trying to attend to many students' needs at once, and there's only one of you (perhaps two, if you happen to have an assistant or co-teacher). Time restraints also limit the amount of differentiation you can provide. In this model, less advanced students might not get enough practice with skills so that they can achieve true proficiency, because the class is already moving on to the next skill. Students might also have skill gaps that are not thoroughly addressed (concepts taught in previous grades, for example). However, students who are more advanced might not experience the level of challenge they need in order to meet their potential for growth. The differentiation options we've discussed in this chapter can help safeguard against these issues to a certain extent, but with whole-class instruction, there's still potential for students to fall through the cracks.

Additionally, this model can make it more difficult to assess students on an ongoing basis. When you're managing all of your students in the same 20- or 30- minute block of instruction, it can be hard to find time to sit and listen to a child read a list of words or an entire text. You might not understand your students' abilities as well as you would in a model based on small-group instruction.

Here are some recommendations to address the possible pitfalls of the whole-group model:

- Enlist as much help as possible. If you can have an assistant teacher or volunteer in your classroom, ask them to come during your phonics block. They can help you maximize instructional time by passing out materials, or even by providing personalized attention to students who need additional support.

- Build differentiation into your routines to create consistency for yourself and for your students. For example, use word sorts on a weekly basis and commit to yourself that you will create at least two versions of the sort for purposes of differentiation. Or you might commit to having one group of students (most frequently, your lowest-performing group) read the decodable text while sitting at the small-group table with you, while the other students read their text independently. The more you can make differentiation a part of your regular routine, the less it will feel like something extra that you're tempted to skip if you're short on time.

- Incorporate assessments that can easily be given in a whole-group setting. You can collect student work on a weekly dictation, for example, to measure their mastery of word spelling with the weekly skill. To assess word reading, you might have students draw a quick sketch or circle the correct picture to show that they have correctly read and understood a word. These whole-group assessments do not take the place of one-on-one assessments and anecdotal notes, but they can still provide valuable information to guide your differentiation efforts.

Above all, remember that no model is perfect—not this one, nor the models described in Chapters 4 and 5. Also, the whole-class model with differentiation looks different in different classrooms. You might be able to add in some small groups to supplement your core, whole-group instruction. Although it has its limitations, the whole-group model is an excellent, efficient way to provide high-quality phonics instruction to all your students. The longer you use this model, the easier it will become to differentiate and attend to your students' varying needs.

What's Next

Now that we've examined how differentiation can be woven into whole-group instruction, we'll next discuss an alternative approach: leveraging small groups for core phonics instruction.

Reference

Sloane, S., Baillargeon, R., & Premack, D. (2012). Do infants have a sense of fairness? *Psychological Science*, 23(2), 196–204. https://doi.org/10.1177/0956797611422072

CHAPTER FOUR

Model 2
Daily Phonics-Focused Small Groups

In the second model, students receive most (but not necessarily all) of their phonics instruction in a small-group setting. Here, you are still using the same scope and sequence with all students, but each group of students is typically working at a different point on the scope and sequence. This model allows for a high level of differentiation, because students are working on the most relevant skills for their current levels of development.

Let's take a peek at how this might play out in a kindergarten classroom and a split first- and second-grade classroom.

Discussion of Mrs. Chau's Kindergarten Classroom

Mrs. Chau chooses to introduce and practice new skills in a small-group setting because she feels that it is the best option for delivering just-right instruction to all of her students. All her students are moving along on the same scope and sequence that goes from the alphabet to digraphs to CVC words, but they are at different points in that sequence and working at different paces.

Some of her students spend most of the year working on letter names and sounds, and they only begin CVC words toward the end of the school year. Other students who have mastered the alphabet during the first few months of whole-group instruction begin working on CVC

CASE STUDY

Mrs. Chau's Kindergarten Classroom

Mrs. Chau gathers her kindergarten students together on the rug to begin their phonics lesson. "Let's start with our warm-up," Mrs. Chau says. She leads students in two minutes of phonemic awareness activities, in which students practice blending and segmenting sounds in three-sound words. Next, Mrs. Chau spends about a minute going through letter flashcards with her students. She holds up a card and students say the letter name and sound (e.g., "B, /b/"). Because she has already taught blending, segmenting, and the alphabet to the entire class, these warm-up activities serve as a review.

Then, Mrs. Chau introduces a new high-frequency word to the class (*she*). She presents students with an example sentence with the word and has them turn to a partner to make up their own sentences with the word. This is all done orally. Mrs. Chau next shows students how the sounds in the word (/sh/ /ē/) are related to the way the word is spelled, with a digraph and vowel. With Mrs. Chau's help, students spell the word aloud while tapping on their arms, and they practice writing the word in a sensory material.

These activities (the warm-up and high-frequency word instruction) usually take between 8 and 10 minutes total. However, Mrs. Chau does not introduce a new high-frequency word every day. At this point, Mrs. Chau tells the class that it is time to break apart into groups for centers. Fifteen of her students move into independent activity stations, and Mrs. Chau sits down at the small-group table with seven students. At the table, Mrs. Chau

holds up a flashcard with the lowercase *o* on it. "What is the name of this letter? What is the sound of this letter?" Students reply with the letter name and sound. "As you already know, the letter *o* is a vowel, and we see it in the middle of some words, like this one." Mrs. Chau holds up a card with the word *hop*. "Listen and watch while I blend to read this word. /h/ /ŏ/, /hŏ/ /p/. What's the word?" Students reply with *hop*. "Great job!" says Mrs. Chau. "Now let's read some other words with short *o*." She guides students in reading five additional words, encouraging the students to do as much of the decoding as possible.

"Now let's build some words with short *o*." Mrs. Chau passes out individual sets of magnetic letters to the seven students. "Our first word is *job*. Say *job*." Students repeat the word. "My job is teaching kindergarten. Tell me the sounds in *job*." Students reply, "/j/ /ŏ/ /b*." Mrs. Chau asks students to build the word using their magnetic letters. Once students are finished, she asks them to check their work by tapping it back. As students point underneath each letter they chose, they say the letter's sound and then the entire word: "/j/ /ŏ/ /b, job*." One student fixes her work. Mrs. Chau shows students the correct spelling on her own set of magnetic letters, and another child adjusts his spelling accordingly. Once again, students tap back the word, "/j/ /ŏ/ /b, job." Mrs. Chau has them clear their boards and build four more short *o* words, one at a time.

Ordinarily, Mrs. Chau would have time for an additional activity with this small group (such as reading decodable sentences or stories), but because she introduced a new high-frequency word earlier in the lesson, it is time to move on. She wraps up the lesson, dismisses those seven students to work independently, and welcomes another seven students to her small-group table for their lesson. This small group is still working on mastering the letter names and sounds, so their lesson includes a BINGO game for review, focused work on the letter *Ww*, and multisensory tracing of alphabet letters. She also models how to decode two CVC (consonant-vowel-consonant) words with *w* (*win, wag*).

During the last rotation, Mrs. Chau works with a group of eight students who are learning the *sh* digraph. Students work together to complete a picture sort of *sh* and *ch* words. They build a few words with *sh* and practice blending to read each word after they have built it.

This concludes the time that Mrs. Chau has allotted for phonics and small groups (50 minutes), so students clean up and move onto the next activity.

words about halfway through the school year. Still others have entered kindergarten already knowing most of or all of their letter names and sounds, and they spend the year working on CVC words, consonant blends, and silent *e* words. Mrs. Chau finds that it is easiest to meet this big range of needs by doing most of her phonics instruction in that small-group setting. She wishes that she could reduce the size of her groups so that they would be a bit easier to manage. However, she knows that it is important for each child to have phonics instruction daily, and she hasn't found it workable to have more than three groups due to the amount of time it would require the other students to work independently.

It's important to note that Mrs. Chau still leverages whole-group instruction when she feels that she can effectively and efficiently address a concept with all of her students. She knows that teaching or practicing the same skill multiple times in different small groups can be time-consuming and inefficient. For example, Mrs. Chau knows that all students benefit from phonemic awareness instruction in blending and segmenting, as well as from reviewing letters to build fluency, so she does these activities with the entire class at the beginning of her lessons (as well as additional phonemic awareness activities sprinkled throughout the day). She still works on phonemic awareness with her small groups, but she can spend less time on these skills because she is

CASE STUDY

Ms. Abazi's First- and Second-Grade Classroom

Ms. Abazi asks her first- and second-grade students to take a seat on the rug. She has students orally segment each of the following words, one at a time: *cap, beach, fled, prop, twist, stamp.* Some of the words with five phonemes (*twist, stamp*) are a bit challenging for her first-grade students, but she likes to include a range of difficulty levels so that her second-grade students are challenged. Next, Ms. Abazi reminds her students of their tasks for independent time, and she dismisses them to begin working. She calls seven of her students (a mix of first and second graders) to the small-group table.

"Friends, do you know what the sound of long *a* is?" Ms. Abazi asks. The students reply, "/ā/." "Yes! We've already talked about how to spell long *a* with a silent *e*. But there are other ways to spell the long *a* sound, and today we're going to learn one of them." She holds up a poster that shows the letters *ai* (see Figure 4.1) and a picture for *rain*. "The letters *a* and *i* can

work together as a vowel team to represent the long /ā/ sound. Let's hold up our fingers and air-write while we say, '*a-i* says /ā/.' Ready?" Ms. Abazi leads students in this quick multisensory activity.

Next, Ms. Abazi writes the word *paid* on a whiteboard. "Let's say each sound and blend to read the word." With Ms. Abazi tracking her finger under the letters, students say, "/p/ /ā/ /d/, paid." Together, they read another word: *main.* Next, Ms. Abazi passes out word lists to the students. Independently, they each whisper-read a list of 10 words that contain *ai.* Ms. Abazi monitors students' progress and provides support when needed.

Ms. Abazi then passes out sets of magnetic letters, one for each student. She has students use them to spell a series of words: *laid, raid, rain, grain, train.* Ms. Abazi does not have them clear their boards each time; rather, she asks students to consider how they would change the current

FIGURE 4.1 Key word poster for the *ai* vowel team.

word to make the next word (e.g., to change *laid* to *raid*, they would replace the *l* with an *r*).

The group's final activity is to begin reading a decodable passage with many *ai* words. Ms. Abazi displays the text, *Snails*, and reads the title to students. She asks students to consider if this passage will be fiction or nonfiction, and why. She also has students turn to the person sitting next to them and share any information that they already know about snails. Afterward, a few students briefly share their thoughts with the group. "Let's look for *ai* words before we read the text," says Ms. Abazi. She passes out copies of the passage and highlighters, and students quickly scan the text for words with the *ai* vowel team, highlighting all the words they find. "Great job!" says Ms. Abazi. "Now, when you see those words in the text, you'll think to yourself, the *a* and *i* are working together to represent the /$\bar{a}$/ sound, and then you'll blend to read the word. Ready

to read?" Students begin whisper-reading the text to themselves. Ms. Abazi listens in and coaches students on their decoding. After a few minutes of reading, Ms. Abazi asks students to stop and discuss what they have learned about snails so far. She also writes an *ai* word on the whiteboard, because she noticed that some students struggled with it, and they decode it together, as a group. Ms. Abazi's time with this small group has ended, so she promises students that they will be able to finish reading the text the following day. Ms. Abazi dismisses the students to work independently, and she calls the next group to her table.

By the time her phonics and small-group block has ended, Ms. Abazi has worked with all of her students, three groups total. Her first group learned about the *ai* vowel team, another group worked on consonant blends with *r*, and another group practiced breaking up multisyllabic words.

covering them in a whole-group setting. Mrs. Chau also chooses to teach the same high-frequency words to her entire class, because she finds that this is efficient and effective. She can review high-frequency words with small groups who need extra practice or occasionally teach a new word to a group of more advanced students.

Discussion of Ms. Abazi's First- and Second-Grade Classroom

Ms. Abazi's students have a wide range of needs, and she feels that she is best able to meet those needs by implementing all her phonics instruction in a small-group setting. Although her groups often engage in many of the same types of activities (e.g., word reading, word building, reading decodable texts), the skills they are working on are tailored to their current levels of phonics development. Just like Mrs. Chau, Ms. Abazi is following a scope and sequence of skills; her groups are simply at different points in the scope and sequence and moving along at different paces.

Ms. Abazi has three different phonics groups in her class, although she wishes she had more time each day for phonics instruction so that she could break up her students into four or even five groups. She has no significant problems managing the children's behavior, but she knows that some of her students' skill levels aren't quite the right fit for their group. For example, in her group of students who are working on the *ai* vowel team, she has one student who still hasn't fully mastered silent *e* words, and another student who already has a high level of mastery with multiple vowel teams. However, neither of these students would be a perfect fit for her other two groups, so Ms. Abazi does the best she can by placing them into their current small group. Ms. Abazi feels that even though her groupings aren't perfect, this is still much better for students than if she tried to teach phonics in a whole-group setting. Ms. Abazi uses weekly dictations and end-of-unit phonics assessments to monitor her students' progress, and sometimes she is able to move a student into a new group.

Although Ms. Abazi implements phonics small groups, this does not mean that she never addresses phonics concepts in a whole-group setting. When she is working through grade-level text with her students, she points out phonics patterns and asks students to help her decode certain words. She also models how she applies phonics knowledge to writing, a subject that she teaches to the entire class simultaneously.

In addition to her phonics small groups, Ms. Abazi also meets with students for skill-based small groups on comprehension and fluency skills. For example, she might pull together a group of students who all need to work on making inferences. In these cases, she uses a text that they can all decode, or she does the reading for them. Ms. Abazi usually only has time for one skill-based small group per day, but she likes to fit them in as much as possible, because her main small-group time is primarily dedicated to phonics skills.

Which Activities Are Best for Small-Group Instruction?

As you've seen from these two example classrooms, any type of phonics activity can be implemented in a small-group setting—from blending practice to word building to decodable text reading. Perhaps a better question is, "Which activities can still be done whole group so that I can focus my small-group time on what matters most?" High-frequency word instruction is a great candidate for whole-group time. Although it's certainly possible to teach high-frequency words in a small-group setting, it can become time-consuming and overwhelming to keep up with the word lists for each group. Phonological awareness exercises (particularly for kindergarten and first grade) are also helpful to complete in a whole-group setting because all students will benefit from it and you can supplement in small groups as needed. Plus, just as Ms. Abazi did when choosing her words for segmenting, you can plan your whole-group lessons to include words or tasks at a range of difficulty levels. Not every task will be the perfect level for each child, but that is simply a natural and acceptable consequence of teaching a diverse class of students.

What Are the Other Students Doing?

In this model, while the teacher pulls small groups of students, the rest of the class must be productively engaged in practicing skills on their own. This sounds great in theory but can be a bit difficult in practice, especially when you're working with young children! Lots of modeling, practice, and setting clear expectations are key, and we will discuss that in more detail in the next section. For now, let's consider the nature of the activities that students will be completing on their own.

When considering the question, "What should the other students be working on?" you'll need to determine if the other students will be practicing only phonics and related skills, or if you also want to incorporate other literacy skills that you're teaching. Many kindergarten and first-grade students need to spend a great deal of their independent time on phonics, phonological awareness, and decoding activities. However, this might also be a time when students (especially those who are reading at least somewhat fluently) can practice other skills that you're teaching throughout your literacy block. For example, students might read with a partner and give each other feedback on their fluency. Students might also work on writing projects during this time or listen to audio books and answer comprehension questions.

When selecting activities, consider the skills students have been working on recently. For instance, if you just finished covering short *a* with a small group, have those students read and/or spell words with short *a* and reread decodable texts with short *a* words. This means that you might want to have different tasks for different groups of students, which you can easily accomplish with color-coded bins or folders. Some tasks (e.g., a writing activity) can be completed by all students, so not all of your independent activities need to be differentiated. Regardless of the task, make sure that students are familiar with it (preferably because they have already done it with you or you have at least modeled it) and that the activity covers skills that students have already been taught. We will discuss independent work differentiation strategies in more detail in Chapter 9.

Another important question is, "How do I structure independent time?" Although there is no single correct way to organize this block of time, here are some logistical considerations:

- Where will students do their activities? Will you have fixed centers or stations throughout the classroom, or will children bring materials to their seats?

- How will you set up groups? Will students work in partners, small groups, alone, or a combination?

- If you're using partner or group work, will students work in similar-ability or mixed-ability groups?

- How will students know which center to visit or which activities to complete?

- How will students change activities or rotate between centers?

- How will you ensure that students are doing what they are supposed to be doing during independent work time?

There is a lot to think about here, and there's not typically a right or wrong answer to these questions. Sometimes testing out an organizational system is the only way to determine if it works for you!

How to Launch Small Groups

Getting started with small groups—whether it's at the beginning of the school year or later on—can feel like the most difficult part. Just like there is no one correct way to organize your small groups and independent work, there's no one right way to launch it, either. However, following these six steps before you launch (or relaunch) small-group and independent work can make the process less overwhelming for you and for your students:

1. **Make decisions about what will happen during this time block.** Before you can plan anything else, you'll need to get clear on what all students will be doing (both in small groups and independent work), what your expectations are for their behavior, how they will change activities, and so on. Refer to the list of questions to consider in the previous section.

2. **Choose a handful of activities that you'd like students to complete as they work independently.** Make sure to select activities that students can do more than once. For example, you might choose the

following for your first-grade students: phonics board games, rereading decodable texts from small-group activities, mapping and building high-frequency words with magnetic letters, writing activities that use target phonics words, and partner reading. This set of activities does not need to encompass all of the tasks you will use throughout the year; this is simply a starting point.

3. **Teach each of the activities you selected to the entire class.** Start with one activity (e.g., a certain type of phonics board game) and set aside 15–20 minutes for a lesson on it. With a student volunteer's help, model how to complete the activity as all students watch. With the board game example, you might place the board game under a document camera so that the other children can watch you and the volunteer go through a few turns of the game. Discuss relevant expectations for the activity, including how to get out and store materials, what students' behavior and voice levels should be like, and so on. In the board game example, you might show students where to find playing pieces and a die, how to decide who goes first, how to roll the die softly so it stays on the table, how to read a word out loud when you land on it, and what to say to yourself if you don't win (e.g., "It's okay; it's just a game and we play for fun and learning"). After you and the volunteer have modeled how to complete the activity, it's time for all students to practice. If you have enough materials for the entire class to practice at the same time, give students 5 to 10 minutes to practice simultaneously. If you don't have enough resources for everyone to practice at the same time, you can allow half or a third of the class to practice while the other children complete something simple, like a handwriting worksheet. Make sure to point out what you notice students doing well; positive reinforcement will help solidify students' understanding of how to do the activity. Once you feel that students are proficient with the activity, you can move on to the next activity. Using this process, you would likely only teach one to two activities each day. You can do this during the block of time that will eventually be reserved for small-group and independent work.

The process of teaching different activities will take place over a couple of weeks, until students know a variety of activities that they can eventually complete during independent work time.

4. **Teach students the logistics of independent work time.** In this step, you'll shift from teaching specific activities to teaching general procedures related to working independently. For example, you might need to teach students how and when they should move from one activity to another, how to look at a choice board or menu to determine what they can work on, what your clean-up signal will be, what to do if they need to use the restroom, and so on. You will already have made decisions about these procedures during step 1, so this is when you communicate those expectations to students. Just like in step 3, you'll want to physically model each procedure, rather than simply talking to students about what you expect. For example, if students are required to move from one table to another as part of center rotations, you'll demonstrate how to get up safely, push in their chairs, and use their walking feet to travel to their next location. You can also invite a student volunteer to model the procedure for the class. Next, have all students in the class practice. You'll repeat this process for every procedure required for independent work. This stage of instruction could be completed in a day or two, 20 to 25 minutes of practice per day. However, for younger students, it might require 10 to 20 minute practice sessions over multiple days or a week. You can also consider setting up mock independent work time as you practice. In mock independent work time, children practice the physical rotations and logistical procedures you're teaching, but they complete simple activities like puzzles or play with table toys, rather than working on literacy tasks. This helps free up students' attention to focus on logistical procedures, rather than asking them to learn these expectations and work productively on academic activities at the same time.

5. **Begin supervised independent work.** In this stage, you'll ask students to combine what they learned in step 3 (the activities) with what they learned in step 4 (procedures and logistics). Students will begin working

independently on the tasks you've taught them. However, you won't pull small groups yet! During this stage, you can tell students that you will be standing back and watching, but they are not to come up and ask you questions. You want to see that students can work as independently as possible so that when you do begin pulling small groups, students will not interrupt you. As you observe students, you can make some notes: both positive praise and reminders that you want to cover after work time is over. During this stage, you don't necessarily need to have students work independently for as long as they eventually will. For example, if your independent work block will be 45 minutes long, you can start with just 20 to 30 minutes at first. After students work independently and have cleaned up, gather them together. Point out what you saw students doing well (and name specific students!) and give some reminders about things you saw not going as intended (but do not name specific students). This stage can be brief, but do not move on to the next stage until you see that students are able to, for the most part, work on their own.

6. **Begin pulling small groups!** Once you see that students can work independently without your direct supervision, you can begin working with small groups of students while the others work independently.

This six-step process might sound lengthy, and you might be tempted to skip over components in the interest of getting to small-group instruction more quickly. However, this set-up time is time well spent. It's important to protect that valuable small-group time from interruption, especially if this is when your students are receiving most of their phonics instruction. When students know what to do and can work on their own, they are less likely to ask for your attention as you try to focus on the small group in front of you.

That said, children are imperfect humans, just like us adults! Sometimes it will be necessary to go back and review expectations. You'll also need to teach additional independent activities throughout the school year. Therefore, even though this six-step process will set you up for success, plan to revisit and reteach procedures throughout the school year as needed. You'll also want to plan ahead for certain days of the year (e.g., after a long break like winter vacation) when review of expectations will be especially important for students' success.

Putting It All Together: Example Schedules

Now let's discuss the practical side of what this might look like on a daily and weekly basis. Here, we'll look at four example schedules: for kindergarten (best for mid-year or later) (Table 4.1), first grade (Table 4.2), second grade (Table 4.3), and third grade (Table 4.4). Note that the overall amount of time allotted for these activities (50 to 60 minutes daily for K–2; 45 to 50 minutes for third) is greater than what you saw in the first model for whole-group instruction. This is because many teachers have time in their schedules for small-group instruction as well as for phonics instruction, and these schedules combine both time blocks. However, these schedules are just a starting point and can be modified. You can likely still use this model if you have slightly less time available.

One word of caution: the amount of time that is designated for text reading on these schedules will not provide enough practice for students who are beyond an early to mid-first-grade reading level. You can ensure that students get enough reading practice by designating focused time for independent reading (of texts that are appropriate for students' skill levels); adding additional, reading-focused small groups as time permits; and/or extending your small-group time to allow for more reading practice. You might also find that, as students master more phonics skills, you can spend less time practicing individual word reading and more time having them read complete texts.

Although these schedules show you doing the same activities with each group, in reality, you might be introducing a new skill to group 1, while reviewing a previously taught skill with group 2 that same day. Small-group instruction gives you this flexibility! You might also have noticed that the routines within these schedules are the same as the

Table 4.1 Kindergarten Sample Schedule with Differentiation Model 2

Monday	Tuesday	Wednesday	Thursday	Friday
Whole Group • Phonological awareness warm-up (2–3 minutes) • Review activities: sounds on flashcards, high-frequency word flashcards (3 minutes) **Activities for Each of Three Small Groups (10–15 mins each)** • Introduce new concept or target letter and review additional letters (3–4 minutes) • Multisensory writing with new skill and review (2–3 minutes) • Blending drill to read words with new skill OR activities / games to practice the target letter and review additional letters (3–4 minutes) • Word building with new skill or practice writing alphabet letters (5 minutes)	**Whole Group** • Phonological awareness warm-up (2–3 minutes) • Review activities: sounds on flashcards, high-frequency word flashcards, blending drill (4 minutes) • Introduce new high-frequency word (5 minutes) **Activities for Each of Three Small Groups (10–15 mins each)** • Read words with Monday's new skill OR activities to review Monday's target letter and review additional letters (3 minutes) • Spell words or letter sounds on whiteboards with Monday's new skill (4–5 minutes) • Read decodable text with Monday's new skill OR picture sort (4–7 minutes)	**Whole Group** • Phonological awareness warm-up (2–3 minutes) • Review activities: sounds on flashcards, high-frequency word flashcards (3 minutes) **Activities for Each of Three Small Groups (10–15 mins each)** • Introduce new concept or target letter (3 minutes) • Multisensory writing with new skill and review (2–3 minutes) • Blending drill to read words with new skill OR games and activities to review alphabet letters (3–4 minutes) • Word building with new skill or practice writing alphabet letters (5 minutes)	**Whole Group** • Phonological awareness warm-up (2–3 minutes) • Review activities: sounds on flashcards, high-frequency word flashcards, blending drill (4 minutes) • Optional: handwriting practice (3–10 minutes) **Activities for Each of Three Small Groups (10–15 mins each)** • Read words with Wednesday's new skill OR activities to review Wednesday's target letter and review additional letters (3 minutes) • Spell words or letter sounds on whiteboards with Monday's new skill (4–5 minutes) • Read decodable text with Wednesday's new skill OR work on oral language and vocabulary OR picture sort (4–7 minutes)	**Whole Group** • Phonological awareness warm-up (2–3 minutes) • Review activities: sounds on flashcards, high-frequency word flashcards, blending drill (3–4 minutes) **Activities for Each of Three Small Groups (10–15 mins each)** • Dictation (7–10 minutes) • Reread decodable texts from this week and play games (5+ minutes)

Table 4.2 First-Grade Sample Schedule with Differentiation Model 2

Monday	Tuesday	Wednesday	Thursday	Friday
Whole Group	**Whole Group**	**Whole Group**	**Whole Group**	**Whole Group**
• Phonological awareness warm-up (2–3 minutes)	• Phonological awareness warm-up (2–3 minutes)	• Phonological awareness warm-up (2–3 minutes)	• Phonological awareness warm-up (2–3 minutes)	• Phonological awareness warm-up (2–3 minutes)
• Review activities: sounds on flashcards, high-frequency word flashcards (3 minutes)	• Review activities: sounds on flashcards, high-frequency word flashcards, blending drill (4 minutes)	• Review activities: sounds on flashcards, high-frequency word flashcards (3 minutes)	• Review activities: sounds on flashcards, high-frequency word flashcards, blending drill (4 minutes)	• Review activities: sounds on flashcards, high-frequency word flashcards, blending drill (3–4 minutes)
Activities for Each of Three Small Groups (15 mins each)	• Introduce new high-frequency word(s) (5 minutes)	**Activities for Each of Three Small Groups (15 mins each)**	• Optional: handwriting practice (3–10 minutes)	**Activities for Each of Three Small Groups (15 mins each)**
• Introduce new concept/skill (3 minutes)	**Activities for Each of Three Small Groups (15 mins each)**	• Introduce new concept/skill (3 minutes)	**Activities for Each of Three Small Groups (15 mins each)**	• Dictation (8–10 minutes)
• Multisensory writing with new skill and review (2–3 minutes)	• Read words with Monday's new skill (3 minutes)	• Multisensory writing with new skill and review (2–3 minutes)	• Word reading with Wednesday's new skill (2–3 minutes)	• Reread decodable texts from this week (7+ minutes)
• Blending drill with new skill (3–4 minutes)	• Spell words on whiteboards with Monday's new skill (4–5 minutes)	• Blending drill with new skill (3 minutes)	• Sort and write (5–7 minutes)	
• Word building with new skill (5 minutes)	• Read decodable text with Monday's new skill (4–7 minutes)	• Word building with new skill (4 minutes)	• For students who are able: practice dividing and reading multisyllabic words with this week's new skills (5 minutes)	
		• Introduce word sort to compare Monday's skill with today's new skill (2- to 3-minute introduction; students can work on the sort as independent work)	• Read decodable text with Wednesday's new skill (4–10 minutes)	

Table 4.3 Second-Grade Sample Schedule with Differentiation Model 2

Monday	Tuesday	Wednesday	Thursday	Friday
Whole Group • Review activities: sounds/patterns, high-frequency words (2–3 minutes) • Optional: phonological awareness warm-up (2–3 minutes) **Activities for Each of Three Small Groups (15 mins each)** • Introduce new skill (2–3 minutes) • Read words with the new skill (3 minutes) • Multisensory writing with new skill and review (2–3 minutes) • Word building with new skill (4–5 minutes)	**Whole Group** • Review activities: sounds/patterns, high-frequency words (2–3 minutes) • Optional: phonological awareness warm-up (2–3 minutes) • Introduce new high-frequency word(s) (5 minutes) **Activities for Each of Three Small Groups (15 mins each)** • Review Monday's new skill; read one-syllable and multisyllabic words with the new skill (3 minutes) • Whiteboard dictation (4–5 minutes) • Read decodable text with Monday's new skill (7–8 minutes; more if time allows)	**Whole Group** • Review activities: sounds/patterns, high-frequency words (2–3 minutes) • Optional: phonological awareness warm-up (2–3 minutes) **Activities for Each of Three Small Groups (15 mins each)** • Introduce new skill (2–3 minutes) • Read words with the new skill (3 minutes) • Multisensory writing with new skill and review (2 minutes) • Word building with new skill (4–5 minutes) • Introduce word sort to compare Monday's skill with today's new skill (2- to 3-minute introduction; students can work on the sort immediately or later on)	**Whole Group** • Review activities: sounds/patterns, high-frequency words (2–3 minutes) • Optional: phonological awareness warm-up (2–3 minutes) • Optional: handwriting practice (3–10 minutes) **Activities for Each of Three Small Groups (15 mins each)** • Sort and write with Monday's and Wednesday's new skills (4–5 minutes) • Practice breaking up and decoding multisyllabic words (4 minutes) • Read decodable text with Wednesday's new skill (6–7 minutes; more if time allows)	**Whole Group** • Review activities: sounds/patterns, high-frequency words (2–3 minutes) • Optional: phonological awareness warm-up (2–3 minutes) **Activities for Each of Three Small Groups (15 mins each)** • Dictation (8–10 minutes) • Reread decodable texts from this week (7+ minutes)

Table 4.4 Third-Grade Sample Schedule with Differentiation Model 2

Monday	Tuesday	Wednesday	Thursday	Friday
Activities for Each of Three Small Groups (15 mins each) • Review activities: sounds/patterns, high-frequency words (2 minutes) • Introduce new skill; multisensory writing with new skill (3–5 minutes) • Read one-syllable and/or multisyllabic words with the new skill (3–4 minutes) • Word building with new skill (4–7 minutes)	**Activities for Each of Three Small Groups (15 mins each)** • Review activities: sounds/patterns, high-frequency words (2 minutes) • Review Monday's new skill; read one-syllable and/or multisyllabic words with the new skill (4 minutes) • Whiteboard dictation (4–5 minutes) • Read decodable text with Monday's new skill (5–8 minutes)	**Activities for Each of Three Small Groups (15 mins each)** • Introduce new skill: multisensory writing with new skill (3–5 minutes) • Read one-syllable and/or multisyllabic words with the new skill (3 minutes) • Word building with new skill (4–5 minutes) • Introduce word sort to compare Monday's skill with today's new skill (2- to 5-minute introduction; students can complete the sort as independent work)	**Activities for Each of Three Small Groups (15 mins each)** • Review activities: sounds/patterns, high-frequency words (2 minutes) • Review Wednesday's new skill; read one-syllable and/or multisyllabic words with the new skill (3 minutes) • Sort and write with Monday's and Wednesday's new skills (4–6 minutes) • Read decodable text with Wednesday's new skill (4–6 minutes)	**Activities for Each of Three Small Groups (15 mins each)** • Dictation (8–10 minutes) • Reread decodable texts from this week (7+ minutes)

routines covered in the Model 1 whole-group schedules. Even though the routines are consistent, remember that the small-group setting enables you to make tweaks to those routines that are appropriate for each group of students (in addition to differentiating the actual skills that you are teaching). For example, in some small groups, you might have students build fewer words because you have several English language learners in that group and you want to take a little more time to discuss vocabulary. Or perhaps some of your groups read an entire decodable text in one lesson, but you have other groups read the text over a period of two lessons. Keep the routines relatively consistent among all your groups, but differentiate by covering skills appropriate for each group, varying the amount of time you spend on activities and varying the amount of support you provide different groups of children.

If restricting the number of small groups you teach to three is not possible, or if you have less time in your schedule and cannot see each group every day, let's take a look at some alternative options for schedules. Remember that students, especially in kindergarten, first grade, and second grade, should receive phonics instruction on a daily basis. If you use these alternative schedules, you will need to introduce most skills to the entire class so that students get enough instructional time each day. Therefore, you'll see that whole-class review and instruction is listed prior to small-group instruction. These schedules are actually a combination of Differentiation Model 1 (which we discussed in Chapter 3) and Differentiation Model 2.

First, let's look at an option in which you have three groups, but you only have about 40 minutes total for your phonics and small-group instruction (see Table 4.5). In this schedule, group 1 is the lowest group, so these students are seen every day by the teacher. You can still use the five-day rotation of activities for groups 2 and 3 that are featured in the previous schedules; it will simply take longer than a week to get to all activities in the rotation because you aren't seeing groups 2 and 3 daily.

Now let's look at an option where you can see three small groups each day, but you have four total groups in your class (see Table 4.6). Again, group 1 is the lowest group, so they are seen every day by the teacher.

Table 4.5 Model 1 and Model 2 Combination Schedule with Two Small Groups Daily

Monday	Tuesday	Wednesday	Thursday	Friday
Whole-class review and instruction (10 mins)	Whole-class review and instruction (10 mins)	Whole-class review and instruction (10 mins)	Whole-class review and instruction (10 mins)	Whole-class review and instruction (10 mins)
Meet with group 1 (15 mins)	Meet with group 3 (15 mins)	Meet with group 1 (15 mins)	Meet with group 3 (15 mins)	Meet with group 1 (15 mins)
Meet with group 2 (15 mins)	Meet with group 1 (15 mins)	Meet with group 2 (15 mins)	Meet with group 1 (15 mins)	Meet with group 2 (15 mins)

Table 4.6 Model 1 and Model 2 Combination Schedule with Three Small Groups Daily

Monday	Tuesday	Wednesday	Thursday	Friday
Whole-class review and instruction (10 mins)	Whole-class review and instruction (10 mins)	Whole-class review and instruction (10 mins)	Whole-class review and instruction (10 mins)	Whole-class review and instruction (10 mins)
Meet with group 1 (15 mins)	Meet with group 4 (15 mins)	Meet with group 3 (15 mins)	Meet with group 4 (15 mins)	Meet with group 3 (15 mins)
Meet with group 2 (15 mins)	Meet with group 1 (15 mins)	Meet with group 2 (15 mins)	Meet with group 1 (15 mins)	Meet with group 2 (15 mins)
Meet with group 3 (15 mins)	Meet with group 2 (15 mins)	Meet with group 1 (15 mins)	Meet with group 2 (15 mins)	Meet with group 1 (15 mins)

These schedules are simply a starting point, so make adjustments as needed, keeping your target skills in mind above all. In other words, when you make changes to the suggested routines, review your plans to ensure that you are still explicitly and systematically teaching skills (including general and specific word knowledge), following a scope and sequence, working on decoding and encoding, and giving students in- and out-of-context practice.

Organizing Your Physical Space

When small-group instruction is an important part of your day, you'll want to take certain elements into consideration when setting up your classroom. For example, you'll need a space for you to teach and a place for your students to sit during small-group instruction. Many teachers use a small table with chairs or stools. If you don't have one, you could teach small groups with students sitting on the rug, or even move desks together to create a table-like space. Choose a quieter location for your small-group instruction. Quiet is definitely a relative term in a busy classroom, but you can avoid, for example, placing your small-group table right next to a noisier independent work station, like partner reading. You'll also want your teacher chair to be angled toward the students you are working with as well as the other students who are working independently so that you can supervise all children in the classroom and ensure their safety.

The materials that you and your students will use during small groups should be set up to be quickly and easily accessed. Ideally, materials should remain near the small-group table throughout the day so that you don't have to spend time roaming the classroom to gather resources. If students use magnetic letters as they work independently, for example, see if you can obtain additional sets that you can set aside specifically for small-group work. You might choose to have different bins, folders, or boxes for the materials that each group will need (e.g., different sets of decodable texts). Color-coding these storage items can help you quickly and easily find a group's materials. You might even want to have a dedicated small-group binder of lesson plans that remains at the small-group table, again for the purpose of quick and easy access.

Next, consider how to best set up your classroom for the type of independent work model that you chose. If students will move to different locations in the classroom for specific activities, try to keep physical space between quieter activities (e.g., independent reading) and louder activities (e.g., partner games). Your classroom furniture can serve to create separate spaces for centers or stations, but make sure that you can still view all students from your small-group table. For example, you wouldn't want students to get into an altercation behind a bookshelf that you can't see around; this would be unsafe. If students will all be working at their seats rather than in different spots around the room, consider if you will provide options or flexibility (must students remain seated, or can they work on the floor near their desks?). You'll also want to consider noise levels. Sometimes allowing students to spread out a bit, even if you don't have designated locations for activities, can reduce the volume.

Additionally, plan how you will make independent work materials easily accessible for your students. Students need to be able to locate what they need and quickly begin using it so that you aren't using up small-group time to help them take out materials. Many times, your trays or bins for independent work will not be able to remain in the same location where students will be using them (e.g., on tables or in a corner of the classroom) throughout the entire school day. In this case, you can have a designated shelf for materials where students (perhaps group leaders) can bring out materials at the beginning of independent work time. You'll also want to think through how to rotate materials in and out because students will likely not work on the exact same activities throughout the year. You'll need a location in your classroom where you can store materials that are not in use, in addition to the designated spot(s) for student-accessible materials that are needed for current activities.

Strengths and Limitations of This Model

One of the strongest advantages of this small-groups model is the level of differentiation that it enables you to provide. Each small group can be working on a different set of skills. You can also customize your pacing, as some small groups might need more time to master a skill than others do. You'll be able to keep a closer eye on how individual students are performing, too. You can provide corrective feedback to a single child more easily than if you are managing an entire class of students simultaneously.

This model also has the potential to provide you with a greater amount of assessment data from formal and informal assessments. Although students are sitting at the small-group table, you can frequently listen to them read, observe how they spell words on their whiteboards, or have a student read a word list to you. Having this regular influx of data will enable you to further personalize your instruction, helping students make gains quickly.

Despite these advantages, this model comes with some notable drawbacks, too. The first of these disadvantages is related to time. It's important for students to have daily phonics instruction (especially in grades K–2), and some teachers find it difficult to fit multiple small groups into their day. They might not be able to work with all their groups every day, which results in less instructional time for students.

Even if time restraints are not a significant issue, teachers might not feel that they can work with all their groups every day because the rest of the students are not productive when working independently. It can be difficult for young children to stay engaged, work together cooperatively, and use materials appropriately. We don't want independent work to be a waste of time for the other students who are not engaged in your small-group instruction, so the quality of students' independent work time is important to take into consideration.

Another disadvantage is the amount of preparation required on a weekly basis. Teachers using this model will need to prepare different activities for each of their small groups. They will also need to find or create meaningful tasks for students who are working independently. Compared to the first model that leverages whole-group instruction, this model requires more time to get materials ready, especially if you are new to implementing this model.

All of that said, many of these disadvantages can be addressed through careful, intentional planning. Here are four recommendations to address them:

- **Keep your total number of small groups to a minimum.** The number of groups you can reasonably make will depend on your class size, but three is a good number to aim for. I would not recommend going beyond four total groups. Restricting the number of groups has several different benefits. First, it reduces the amount of time you need for small-group instruction, therefore making it easier to fit small groups into your schedule and see each group every day. Additionally, students will be required to spend less time working independently than if you had a larger number of groups to see, which helps cut down on unproductive time. However, if the students in your class have a very diverse range of needs, you might think, "Three groups isn't nearly enough!" Although it would be great to have all students in a small group working at exactly the same level, this isn't realistic for most classrooms. "Good enough" still allows for a high level of differentiation. You can also think in terms of skill bands instead of single skills. For example, perhaps you have some students who need to work on consonant digraphs and others who are working on mastering consonant blends. Although these are two different skills, they fall next to each other on a typical phonics scope and sequence. Therefore, over the course of a week, you might have this group work on words that have digraphs, words that have blends, and words that have both digraphs and blends, thereby meeting the needs of all students in that group. (Of course, you would still plan clear, explicit lessons on both types of phonics patterns.)

- **Break up your small-group block.** Sometimes, teachers find that they can move through three small groups in a row, and students stay productive throughout a 45- to 60-minute block, even when they're not meeting with the teacher. However, other teachers find that students tend to get off-task and do not make the most of independent work time. To deal with this challenge, you can consider adding a break in between small-group rotations. Students can get up, stretch, and/or participate in a movement activity. You could even plan for a different instructional activity to take place between rotations, like a read-aloud or writing time. Taking a break can help students reset and get ready to resume working independently.

- **Choose independent work activities thoughtfully.** With all that you have going on as a teacher, it's easy to fall into the habit of choosing independent work activities at the last minute, cobbling things together to fill students' time. Unfortunately, a consequence of haphazardly selecting materials is that students might not get the most out of independent work time. You might accidentally omit important skills or choose activities that are cute but not substantive. However, when you have an intentional routine for selecting independent activities, this makes it easier to ensure that independent work time is productive and meaningful. To create your routine, make sure you're clear on the skills you want students to practice independently. For example, a kindergarten teacher might create a weekly checklist that includes alphabet recognition, letter sounds, phonemic awareness, fine-motor skills, and applying phonics through invented spelling. A second-grade teacher's checklist might include decoding words and sentences, decoding complete texts, building fluency, spelling words, and practicing comprehension through written response. Once you have your checklist, use it each week to select activities. This will help you ensure that you cover all your intended skills, versus just choosing an activity for each type of center. For example, if you have a partner game station, you could choose a decoding, phonemic awareness, or vocabulary game, depending on the week. Using your checklist will then help you make sure that you cover the other skills in other centers.

- **Enlist the help of volunteers**. Volunteers can support this model in a variety of ways! First, you might have a parent or community volunteer support students who are working independently. They can supervise an activity, help with technology problems, and provide another adult set of hands so that you can focus on working with your small group. Volunteers can also help you prepare materials by sorting, cutting, stapling, making copies, and so on. Some family members of your students might want to volunteer but cannot come to the classroom during school hours, so you can offer to send things home in a folder for them to prepare and return to school. Because this model requires more preparation time, volunteers can help reduce your workload to make it more manageable.

Again, keep in mind that no model is perfect. This model certainly has its challenges, but when implemented effectively, it can be an outstanding approach to differentiating your phonics instruction and meeting a wide range of student needs.

What's Next?

This model for small-group instruction works well for students who are still working on mastering foundational phonics skills. However, what about more advanced students who need less phonics instruction and more time for reading connected text? This is exactly what we will discuss in Chapter 5.

Model 3
Phonics as Part of Reading-Focused Small Groups

Our third and final model is similar to the one described in Chapter 4 in the sense that it involves using small groups as the primary tool for differentiating phonics instruction. However, this third model differs from Model 2 in that, here, the teacher devotes more time in small groups to reading and comprehending text (typically grade level or other leveled text). Compared to Model 2, less time is spent on out-of-context phonics activities like reading individual words.

For this reason, the approach described in this chapter is *only* recommended for use with students who have already achieved a high level of mastery with the essential phonics skills typically included in a K–2 scope and sequence. Students at this stage are reading fluently. They still need instruction in how to break down and decode multisyllabic words. Typically, these students can read more challenging words than what they can spell. For example, they might be able to decode three- and four-syllable words, but they still misspell certain words with vowel teams. Therefore, it's important to continue providing encoding (spelling) instruction that is based on students' strengths and needs.

There are several different ways that this final model might be implemented. Let's take a look at one version of this model in a third-grade classroom.

CASE STUDY

Mrs. Maka's Third-Grade Classroom

Mrs. Maka and her students have just finished a whole-group reading lesson on nonfiction text features and are moving into independent work time. As the rest of the students settle into their assigned independent tasks, Mrs. Maka calls six students over to her small-group table. This group of students is currently meeting third-grade expectations and continuing to work on grade-level skills.

At the table, Mrs. Maka introduces a third-grade-level passage about fossils to the students. She directs students, "Turn to the person sitting next to you and share anything you already know about fossils." After students briefly discuss their prior knowledge with a partner, she calls on two students to share with the group. Next, Mrs. Maka quickly reviews the definition of the term *extinct* with students, explaining that they will learn from the passage how fossils help us learn about extinct creatures. Then, Mrs. Maka directs students to begin silently reading the text. While students read, she checks in with a few students. She asks one student to quietly read aloud for her, and she asks two other students to summarize what they've read so far. After the group finishes reading the passage, Mrs. Maka asks them to take turns retelling the most important information from the text. Mrs. Maka asks students to point out a few key text features from the passage, explain what information they convey, and how that information is connected to the main body text.

The reading and discussion takes about 15 minutes. Mrs. Maka spends the next five minutes having students break apart three-syllable words with the *schwa* sound. First, she writes the word *amazement* on the board, discusses the *schwa* sound for the first *a*, and models how to break the word up into its syllables (*a/maze/ment*). She asks students about the vowel sound in the syllable *maze* and discusses the silent *e* syllable. Students also discuss how the *e* in the final syllable sounds more like a short *i*. Then, Mrs. Maka passes out a list of six words to each student. Every word on the list has three syllables and includes the *schwa* sound. Students begin dividing each word into its syllables, reading the word, and looking for the *schwa* sound. There is not enough time for students to finish, but Mrs. Maka discusses three of the words with students (the syllable division and the meaning of the words) and directs them to finish the sheet during independent work time.

Next, Mrs. Maka pulls another group of students over. They are reading texts that are above current grade-level expectations. She has them read a nonfiction passage and follows a set of procedures similar to the one she used with the on-level group. After students have read and discussed the passage, she works with them on four-syllable words with the *schwa* sound.

When independent work time is over, Mrs. Maka has worked with three different groups on text reading and decoding multisyllabic words. This is what her small-group time looks like for four out of five days of the week.

However, one day each week, Mrs. Maka meets with small groups to introduce differentiated spelling lists (her spelling groups are based on student spelling ability and differ slightly from her reading groups). During that lesson, Mrs. Maka discusses the phonics features of the words and makes sure that students know what the words mean. Students practice their words throughout the week during independent work time. At the end of the week, Mrs. Maka meets with each group to give them each a quick dictation (this takes place outside of her normal small-group time). The information she gets from the dictation helps her decide if she will introduce completely new words or continue reviewing the words from the current week.

Discussion of Mrs. Maka's Third-Grade Classroom

Similar to the teachers in Chapter 4, Mrs. Maka differentiates her phonics instruction by leveraging small-group instruction. She works with each group on decoding words that are at an appropriate difficulty level for their development. Mrs. Maka's selection of words for students to decode are not random; she is moving along a scope and sequence of skills. Similarly, Mrs. Maka bases her spelling instruction on the scope and sequence. Each of her spelling groups is working on a different set of skills in the scope and sequence, and she adjusts her pacing based on student performance on the weekly dictations.

That said, the majority of her small-group time is spent reading and discussing grade-level or other leveled texts, rather than on out-of-context phonics practice and decodable texts. Her students are mostly fluent readers who have achieved a high level of mastery with K–2 phonics skills. Their phonics knowledge serves as an important foundation on which they can build fluency and improve comprehension.

Some years, Mrs. Maka has students in her class who are still working on K–2 phonics skills. When she meets with these groups, she focuses on explicitly teaching skills, having students decode and encode words with the skill, and working with students on decodable texts (similar to the small-group instruction described in Chapter 4). With students who are reading on or above grade level, she spends more time on text reading, comprehension, and multisyllabic word reading, using the approach from this chapter. Of course, all of her students receive additional comprehension instruction in a whole-group setting.

Example Schedules

You'll notice that these example schedules do not have grade levels listed on them; this is intentional. Although this model is designed for students who have mastered K–2 phonics skills, this does not necessarily mean that this model is only for third grade and up. Students might be ready for this model in late second grade or not until fourth grade. Time frames for each activity are simply suggestions and might be adjusted as needed.

Reading Focused Small-Group Schedule with Differentiation Model 3

- Introduce new text: 1–2 minutes

- Read new text: 8–9 minutes

- Retell and discuss text (comprehension): 5–6 minutes; if more in-depth comprehension work is desired, the text reading time can be slightly shortened and this can be lengthened
- Decoding instruction (can also be placed prior to the text introduction): 4–5 minutes

Spelling Small-Group Schedule with Differentiation Model 3 (Once Per Week)

- Introduce spelling pattern and teach rule if applicable; have students decode several words with the pattern: 3–4 minutes

- Dictate one word at a time for students to spell on whiteboards, making sure to discuss each word's meaning: 10–12 minutes
- Give students list of words to practice independently; chorally read all words: 3–4 minutes

Rotation Schedule, Differentiation Model 3

This first example schedule (Table 5.1) matches Mrs. Maka's approach, in which one day is designated for spelling instruction, four days are focused on decoding and comprehension, and Friday has extra time built in for spelling assessment via a dictation. In this example, reading group 1 is the lowest group, which is why they meet with the teacher four times per week. Reading groups 2 and 3 are seen three times weekly, and reading group 4 meets with the teacher twice weekly. There are only three spelling groups, rather than four, to make differentiation easier to implement.

This schedule is only an example and might not match your students' needs or schedule, so feel free to adjust as you see fit. For example, you might not have an extra 20 to 30 minutes on Fridays for differentiated dictation, so you choose to cut down on your reading group time accordingly.

Table 5.1 Example Schedule with Separate Small-Group Spelling and Reading Days

Monday	Tuesday	Wednesday	Thursday	Friday
Meet with spelling group 1 (15–20 mins)	Meet with reading group 1 (20 minutes)	Meet with reading group 4 (20 minutes)	Meet with reading group 3 (20 minutes)	Meet with reading group 2 (20 minutes)
Meet with spelling group 2 (15–20 mins)	Meet with reading group 2 (20 minutes)	Meet with reading group 1 (20 minutes)	Meet with reading group 4 (20 minutes)	Meet with reading group 3 (20 minutes)
Meet with spelling group 3 (15–20 mins)	Meet with reading group 3 (20 minutes)	Meet with reading group 2 (20 minutes)	Meet with reading group 1 (20 minutes)	Meet with reading group 1 (20 minutes)
-	-	-	-	Meet with each spelling group individually for dictation assessment (20–30 mins total)

Variations on This Model

Mrs. Maka's classroom represents one way that this model can be implemented, but there are certainly other options that work well. One of those options is to integrate *decoding instruction* into your reading-focused small groups but teach *spelling* in a whole-group setting. Not meeting with small groups for spelling can save a bit of time, potentially leaving you with more time for small-group reading instruction. Table 5.2 shows what your schedule might look like if you choose this variation.

If you choose this variation, you can use some of the tools described in Chapter 3 for your whole-group spelling instruction. For example,

Table 5.2 Example Schedule with Whole-Group Spelling Instruction and Reading Small Groups

Monday	Tuesday	Wednesday	Thursday	Friday
Whole-group spelling instruction (10 minutes)	Whole-group spelling instruction (10 minutes)	N/A	N/A	Whole-group spelling instruction— assessment (10–20 minutes, depending on if you differentiate assessments)
Meet with reading group 1 (20 minutes)	Meet with reading group 4 (20 minutes)	Meet with reading group 3 (20 minutes)	Meet with reading group 2 (20 minutes)	Meet with reading group 4 (20 minutes)
Meet with reading group 2 (20 minutes)	Meet with reading group 1 (20 minutes)	Meet with reading group 4 (20 minutes)	Meet with reading group 1 (20 minutes)	Meet with reading group 1 (20 minutes)
Meet with reading group 3 (20 minutes)	Meet with reading group 2 (20 minutes)	Meet with reading group 1 (20 minutes)	Meet with reading group 3 (20 minutes)	Meet with reading group 2 (20 minutes)

when teaching students about soft *g*, you have students practice spelling one- and two-syllable soft *g* words with your support. However, the word lists you give students for independent practice are differentiated (e.g., some students work with one-syllable words and other students spell two-syllable words).

A third option is technically different from the title of this model because it completely separates phonics instruction from your reading small groups, but it's still worth consideration for students who have already mastered foundational phonics skills. In this option, you'd see two reading-focused small groups per day and one phonics-focused small group per day. This approach can be helpful because it enables you to focus on one skill set at a time: reading and comprehension during your reading-focused small groups and decoding and encoding (mostly individual words) during your phonics-focused small groups. Table 5.3 shows an example of what this might look like this.

Although this schedule only includes two reading small groups, you could certainly add in another group each day.

In any of these Model 3 options, most of your small-group time is devoted to having students read and discuss grade-level or other

Table 5.3 Example Schedule with Daily Phonics and Reading Small Groups

Monday	Tuesday	Wednesday	Thursday	Friday
Meet with phonics group 1 (20 mins)	Meet with phonics group 2 (20 mins)	Meet with phonics group 3 (20 mins)	Meet with phonics group 1 (20 mins)	Meet with phonics group 2 (20 mins)
Meet with reading group 1 (20 minutes)	Meet with reading group 3 (20 minutes)	Meet with reading group 1 (20 minutes)	Meet with reading group 3 (20 minutes)	Meet with reading group 1 (20 minutes)
Meet with reading group 2 (20 minutes)	Meet with reading group 4 (20 minutes)	Meet with reading group 2 (20 minutes)	Meet with reading group 4 (20 minutes)	Meet with reading group 2 (20 minutes)

leveled text (in comparison to Model 2, where phonics is the primary focus of your small groups). In Model 3, students still receive decoding and encoding instruction that is differentiated for their needs. Even though I have created a divide here between reading-focused and phonics-focused small groups, it's important to keep in mind that there is certainly overlap! When students are reading any text, they are applying phonics knowledge to decode the words. If you notice that students struggle to decode a word as they are reading, take the time to break it apart with them, even if your primary focus for the group is comprehension. Similarly, when students are working with decodable text, they should also be practicing comprehension skills. Take time to have students retell the decodable text after they read it, and ask them comprehension questions to challenge their thinking.

Strengths and Limitations of This Model

As students move beyond K–2 phonics skills, our instructional focus should shift. This model enables teachers to increase their focus on reading comprehension, yet still make time for differentiated decoding and encoding instruction. There is a lot of flexibility within this model, as we saw with the various options and small-group arrangements.

Of course, this model has its drawbacks, too. It can be difficult to implement this model if you have a handful of students who are working on K–2 phonics skills, while the rest of your class is made up of fluent readers. Those students who are, presumably, working below grade level, typically need a great deal of practice time to master phonics skills and build reading fluency. Many times, the schedules in this chapter will not provide enough phonics instructional time for these students, so additional intervention time is necessary.

Another potential trouble spot is the amount of time that students are expected to work independently in this model (about 60 minutes in most of these examples). Procedures and expectations must be carefully taught so that this time is productive; please see the sections in Chapter 4 titled "What Are the Other Students Doing?" and "How to Launch Small Groups" for more details on setting up independent work time. If you find that students are not working productively or staying on task, consider shortening your small-group time and/or breaking up independent work time. For example, you might see two small groups, have the entire class go out to recess or take a movement break, and then return to meet with an additional small group.

As a final reminder, this model should not be implemented with students who do not have a solid phonics foundation. If we rush into spending our small-group time mostly on comprehension when students do not have the decoding skills they need, our efforts will be in vain. Students cannot effectively comprehend text when they struggle to decode many of the words.

What's Next?

Now that we've covered all three models for differentiation, you might have some initial thoughts on the model you'd like to implement. Or you might still be feeling unsure. Either way, the next chapter will provide clarity by comparing the three models, as well as by giving suggestions for choosing a model based on the amount of time you have available and your students' needs.

How to Choose the Model That's Right for You

Now that you've read about each of the three models, you might have an idea about which option is best for you and your students. Before you make a final decision, let's compare and contrast the three models and discuss how you might find the best fit by combining elements of multiple models.

Considerations for Choosing a Model

In Table 6.1, you'll find a visual summary of the key components of each of the three models.

When you're selecting a model, one big consideration is the amount of time you have available. Some schools specify how many minutes you should devote to phonics instruction, and others leave it up to the teacher. To date, the research has yet to identify the perfect number of minutes for phonics instruction, but many schools allot about 30 minutes per day.

That said, to be able to teach phonics in a small-group setting and meet with multiple groups, you would need more than 30 minutes (unless you have a relatively small class). Therefore, if your students are working on K–2 phonics skills and you are allotted less than 45 minutes total for phonics and small-group literacy instruction combined, then the

Table 6.1 Comparison of All Three Models for Differentiation

	Model 1: Whole-Class Instruction with Built-In Differentiation	Model 2: Daily Phonics-Focused Small Groups	Model 3: Phonics in Reading-Focused Small Groups
Phonics instruction is differentiated to meet students' unique needs.	✓	✓	✓
Phonics lessons are taught to the entire class at the same time.	✓	X	X
The entire class is working on the same skill at the same time.	✓	X	X
Phonics lessons are taught to students in similar-ability small groups.	X	✓	✓
Different groups of students are working on different skills.	X	✓	✓
Phonics instruction is an addition to, but not the main focus of, small-group instruction.	X	X	✓
Students are often grouped differently for decoding and encoding instruction.	X	X	✓

whole-group model is likely your best bet. Although it doesn't allow for the same level of differentiation as the small-group models do, whole-group instruction can still be very effective. Depending on how much time you have available, you can likely still incorporate some small-group work even when your core lesson is taught in a whole-group setting. Take a peek back at Chapter 4 to revisit the example schedule that combined a brief, whole-group phonics lesson (10 minutes) with additional small-group instruction.

If, however, you have 45 minutes or more that you can leverage for phonics instruction and small groups, *and* students are still working on kindergarten through second-grade phonics skills, you can choose Model 2, daily phonics-focused small groups. Students at this level need daily phonics instruction so make sure that you meet with every small group each day. If you only have about 45 minutes available to you, you'll likely want to limit your total number of phonics small groups to three or four. If you have 60 minutes or more, you could potentially work with four to five groups. However, keep in mind that 60+ minutes is a long time for the other students to work independently, so you'll want to consider splitting up your small-group time into two shorter blocks.

If you have 45 minutes or more to work with, and your students have already mastered kindergarten through second-grade phonics skills, you can consider Model 3. Even though reading connected text will be the focus of your small-group instruction, you'll want to make sure to follow a scope and sequence for your decoding and encoding instruction to ensure that instruction in these areas is not an afterthought. Students at this level still need phonics instruction to realize their full potential in reading and writing. If you have less than 15 to 20 minutes available to meet with each small group to work on both reading and phonics, you might want to consider teaching a daily or several-times-weekly whole-class phonics lesson, and then reserving your small-group time for reading and comprehension work.

Of course, the amount of time you have available is not the only aspect to consider. Your students' needs will also play a primary role in the model you choose. For example, let's say that you teach first grade, and you have 50 minutes available to you for phonics and small-group instruction. However, all of your students, except for three children, have begun the school year reading CVC (consonant-vowel-consonant) words. They are ready to work on digraphs next. Some children have mastered many of the digraphs, but most students still need work in this area. Therefore, you decide to teach a whole-group phonics lesson for 25 minutes each day, and then work with two small groups per day to reinforce and differentiate the skills taught in your whole-group lessons. In this example, you have chosen Model 1, whole-group instruction with supplementary small-group work, because this is the most efficient way to deliver instruction given your students' relatively homogenous needs. If you had chosen Model 2, you would have ended up teaching the same content over and over in your small groups, which is not the best use of instructional time.

Too Many Needs and Not Enough Time?

Sometimes there will be a conflict between students' needs and the amount of time you have available. In these cases, you have to choose the best possible model, even if it is not a perfect fit. For example, let's say that you're a second-grade teacher who has 40 minutes that you can use for phonics and small-group reading instruction. Your students, many of whom are working below grade level, represent a big range of needs (see the following example). You want to divide students up into four groups to ensure that they are working on the skills most appropriate for their levels. However, if you only have 40 minutes available, this approach is probably not feasible. You would need to meet with each small group for about nine minutes per day, with one minute allotted for transitions. Nine minutes is simply not enough time to teach and practice decoding and encoding, as well as read connected text.

Many teachers (including myself) experience frustration when they find themselves in a similar situation. They can clearly see that students need differentiated instruction, yet they are not given as much instructional time as they feel is required to meet their students' needs. They

Distribution of Student Skill Needs in an Example Second-Grade Classroom

Here are the skills that students are ready to work on next:

Consonant and short vowel sounds (alphabet)

CVC words and plural CVC words

Consonant digraphs

Double final consonants (-*ff*, -*ll*, -*ss*, -*zz*)

Consonant blends—**4 students**

Glued sounds—**5 students**

R-controlled vowels *or*, *ar* (*er*, *ir*, and *ur* might be taught for decoding but are not typically mastered until after students have learned vowel teams)—**2 students**

Silent *e*

Vowel teams—**8 students**

R-influenced vowel patterns (all vowels)—**2 students**

Diphthongs

Complex consonants (silent consonants, three-letter blends, soft *c* and *g*, word endings -*dge*/-*ge* and -*tch*/-*ch*)

Adding -*ing* and -*ed* to one-syllable words where the base word spelling changes

Unaccented syllables with *schwa*

Advanced prefixes and suffixes, including Greek and Latin roots

feel that they are being held back from helping their students reach their full potential, and that's not a good feeling. If this is your situation, the best thing you can do is to accept the difficult situation for what it is, choose an imperfect solution, and trust that students will still move forward with their literacy development.

If we look at the distribution of skill needs in the preceding example, we see a wide range of student needs. But we also see somewhat of a division: students who need to work on consonant blends, glued sounds, and beginning *r*-controlled vowels and students who need to work on vowel teams and *r*-influenced vowel patterns. With 40 minutes to work with in this hypothetical situation, you might say to yourself, "Although I can't divide students up as much as I'd like to, I can put my class into two groups, a lower and higher group, and teach two phonics lessons daily. That will enable me to get closer to students' levels and give me sufficient time to teach my lessons." You would then use a variation of Model 2 to deliver your instruction. For the first 20 minutes of your time block, you meet with the students who need to work on consonant blends, glued sounds, and *r*-controlled vowels. You begin by teaching consonant blends, the easiest skill that students in the group need to work on. You might challenge your higher students by giving them words to decode and encode that contain more than one blend (e.g., the word *stamp*). Or, you could even pull these higher students aside and provide a quick skill introduction for a skill they need to work on. For example, after passing out lists of consonant blend words for students to decode, you might quickly teach *ar* to the two most advanced students in that group. You would then give these students consonant blend words to read that also include *ar* (like *start* and *smart*). This could also be accomplished by giving those students a video about *ar* to watch.

Then, after you meet with your lower phonics group each day, you switch to meeting with your higher group (meanwhile, the lower group works independently on follow-up phonics tasks). You begin working on vowel teams with your higher group. Just like you did with the students who needed to work on *r*-controlled vowels, you look for opportunities for your higher students within that group to work on complex *r*-influenced vowel patterns.

Although the solution I described here isn't perfect, it's still better than trying to teach the same skills to all your students at once, or trying to cram your phonics instruction into nine minutes per day per small group. Most schools are not set up to provide completely personalized instruction to students, so we must do our best within the limitations of our situation (and not be too hard on ourselves). Plus, remember how we discussed the importance of reviewing skills? Having students complete further work on skills that they have already mastered is not a bad thing at all! Kids at this age are sponges and will continue to move forward in their literacy development, even if our instruction is not 100% differentiated all the time.

Blending Multiple Models for Differentiation

As you've probably noticed throughout this chapter and the previous ones, you can use elements of all three models to best suit your schedule and students' needs! Here are just a few examples:

- You teach a whole-class phonics lesson to your first graders (20–25 minutes) and meet with one phonics small group per day for follow-up, differentiated instruction (10–15 minutes).

- In your third grade classroom, you teach spelling in a daily whole-group lesson (5–10 minutes) and teach decoding in differentiated, reading-focused small groups (50 minutes).

- You teach a brief phonics lesson (10 minutes) to all of your kindergarten students on a daily basis, where you teach or review high-frequency words, practice phonological awareness skills, and introduce or review new phonics skills. After the brief lesson, you move into small groups, where you provide practice with the weekly skill and/or work on different skills, depending on what students need. You meet with three small groups per day for 12 minutes each.

As you can see, although I've described three distinct models for differentiating your phonics instruction, in reality, the lines are blurred. Being flexible and incorporating different aspects from multiple models can be helpful in making differentiated phonics instruction work for you and your students!

When to Change Up Your Model

Here's some great news: if you start out using one model and later decide that you'd like to try a different model, that is perfectly fine! Of course, you'll want to give your original model some time before making a decision (ideally, about four to six weeks). Whenever something is new, it will feel clunky at first, and it will take some time for you and your students to adjust to the routines. However, if you've already gone through an adjustment period and still do not feel that the model is the best choice, make changes as you see fit.

You will also want to remain open to making changes based on student performance throughout the year. For example, you might choose to start the school year with the whole-group model for instruction, because your beginning-of-the-year assessment showed that many students in your class have the same needs in phonics. However, after teaching the first two units of your phonics program, you discover that some students have really taken off with their phonics development, and others are not mastering the skills that you've taught so far. You realize that students would be better served through more small-group instruction, so you shift your model. You work on the previously covered phonics skills with your lower groups, continue teaching the next unit with your on-level groups, and move more quickly through the content with your higher groups so that they can begin advanced skill work.

Giving students some kind of post-test for each unit of phonics instruction is extremely important because it enables you to make these kinds of instructional decisions. As we have discussed in other chapters, ongoing assessment (e.g., through dictations) is also important, because it helps you determine if students are ready to move onto the next skill or not. In Table 6.2, you'll find a simple guide to help you determine when to move onto the next skill, and what to do when you find that students do not all perform similarly on an assessment. This guide can be

Table 6.2 If/Then Guide for Determining When to Move On to the Next Skill

If . . .	Then . . .
Less than 60% of students have achieved 80%+ mastery with the target concept(s)	Do not move onto the next skill; review and reinforce the target concept(s)
60% to 95% of students have achieved 80%+ mastery with the target concept(s)	Move onto the next skill, but use small-group instruction and differentiated practice tools with students who did not master the target concept(s)
100% of students have achieved 80%+ mastery with the target concept(s)	Move onto the next skill, and consider accelerating your pacing if the content is easy for students

used when looking at data from a weekly assessment and when reviewing student results on a unit or longer-term assessment.

Whenever you give an assessment, you will likely find that some students are a little behind and other students are a little ahead. This does not necessarily mean that you need to change up your entire model for delivering phonics instruction, but you will want to keep an eye on the gap between student levels of achievement. The larger the gap grows, the more differentiation is needed.

What's Next?

Now that we've covered the core of differentiated phonics instruction and how to select a model, we will discuss how to apply this information when working with two specific groups of students: kindergarten students (or students working at a kindergarten level) and students who are learning English as an additional language. Feel free to skip either or both of these chapters (7 and 8) if they do not apply to you. If you prefer to go directly to Chapter 9, there you will find suggestions for differentiating phonics activities that students complete independently, outside of your main phonics lessons.

Special Considerations for Early Kindergarten

As a former kindergarten teacher, I can attest to the fact that kindergarten is unique! This is true from an instructional standpoint, as well as from behavioral and social-emotional perspectives. Therefore, although you will be able to use many of the ideas shared in the previous chapters, the beginning of the year in kindergarten deserves special attention because phonics instruction looks very different than it does at other grade levels. In this chapter, I'll share my best recommendations, based on research and my own experiences, on how to structure your phonics instruction as a kindergarten teacher and how to appropriately differentiate.

Please note that when I refer to *kindergarteners* in this book, I'm referring to children who are ready to learn the alphabet and then begin reading simple words. In the United States, most children turn five prior to or just after beginning kindergarten. Some kindergarten children are six years old. I recognize that the nature of kindergarten differs from country to country.

Teaching the Alphabet

Most kindergarten teachers' phonics instruction starts with the alphabet. In North America, teachers commonly progress through a sequence of the consonant and short vowel letter names, sounds, and letter formation (how to write the letters). This instruction usually takes place toward the beginning of the school year. Depending on how quickly the letters are taught and learned, alphabet instruction might take anywhere from a few months to most of the school year.

Although teaching the alphabet might seem like a straightforward task at first glance, students' unique needs can present some challenges and complications. Children in a single kindergarten class might enter school with no letter knowledge, some letter knowledge, or even the ability to read (Remember my student Heidi, from the Introduction?) Teachers often wonder, "Is it a waste of time to teach my students the letters, when many students already know some or all of them?"

Unless all the students in your class have mastered the letter names and letter sounds, there is, indeed, plenty of value in covering the alphabet. Here are five principles to follow to make alphabet instruction a valuable experience for all your students:

- Assess students toward the beginning of the school year so that you can adapt your instruction accordingly. If there are letters for which all students (or the vast majority) can produce the letter name and sound, plan to spend less time on these letters. However, make sure to dedicate time to teaching letter formation. Even kindergarten students who are already reading often need instruction in this area.

- Introduce a letter's name and sound at the same time (Piasta & Wagner, 2010). There's no need to teach all the letter names and then go back and teach the letter sounds.

- Cover more than one letter per week (Stahl, 2014). If you teach only one letter per week, you potentially spend large amounts of time covering letters that some (or many) children already know. Plus, students best learn the alphabet through frequent exposure and repetition of the letters (e.g., Justice et al., 2006; McBride-Chang, 1999). Focusing solely on one letter per week does not provide sufficient repetition, when compared to instruction that covers the letters more quickly and then loops back for review.

- Incorporate phonemic awareness into your alphabet instruction, especially activities that require students to identify, contrast, and match beginning sounds (Mesmer, 2019).
- Provide extra challenges for students who need them. In the section on differentiating your alphabet instruction, we will cover plenty of examples of what this can look like in practice.

Suggested Schedule

There are many different ways to effectively teach the alphabet. The example schedule provided in Table 7.1 follows the research by teaching letter names and sounds together, incorporating phonological awareness instruction, reviewing previously taught letters, and helping students develop an understanding of the alphabetic principle. Feel free to adjust this schedule or substitute different activities. You'll notice that, in this schedule, high-frequency word activities are listed as optional. I do not recommend beginning high-frequency word instruction with kindergarten students until they have mastered at least a handful of letter sounds. Letters and sounds are the building blocks of learning to read so it makes sense to focus on them first before adding in high-frequency words.

Should I Teach the Alphabet in Small Groups?

If you assess your students at the beginning of the school year and find that students vary widely in terms of their alphabet knowledge, you might wonder, "Should I skip whole-group alphabet instruction and teach it in a small-group setting instead?" Although it might be tempting to dive right into small groups at the beginning of the school year, there are several factors that lead me to recommend waiting six to eight weeks before you begin small-group instruction in kindergarten.

First, the beginning of the school year is an adjustment period for many kindergarten students. For some children, this is their first

Table 7.1 Example Schedule for Teaching the Alphabet

Monday	Tuesday	Wednesday	Thursday	Friday
• Phonological awareness warm-up (2–3 minutes) • Review activities: letter names and/or sounds on flashcards, high-frequency word flashcards if applicable, blending drill with support (3 minutes) • Introduce new alphabet letter: read aloud a rhyme, brainstorm words that begin with the letter, teach chant for the letter (4–5 minutes) • Picture sound sort with the new letter (10–15 minutes) • Optional: Teach new high-frequency word (3–4 minutes)	• Phonological awareness warm-up (2–3 minutes) • Review activities: letter names and/or sounds on flashcards, high-frequency word flashcards if applicable, blending drill with support (2–3 minutes) • Alphabet video and movement (2 minutes) • Optional: high-frequency word writing (3–4 minutes) • Read letter book with new letter from Monday (2 minutes) • Teach and practice letter formation: handwriting with new letter from Monday (10–16 minutes)	• Phonological awareness warm-up (2–3 minutes) • Review activities: letter names and/or sounds on flashcards, high-frequency word flashcards if applicable, blending drill with support (3 minutes) • Introduce new alphabet letter: read aloud a rhyme, brainstorm words that begin with the letter, teach chant for the letter (4–5 minutes) • Picture sound sort with the new letter (10–15 minutes)	• Phonological awareness warm-up (2–3 minutes) • Review activities: letter names and/or sounds on flashcards, high-frequency word flashcards if applicable, blending drill with support (2–3 minutes) • Alphabet video and movement (2 minutes) • High-frequency word practice (3–4 minutes) • Read letter book with new letter from Wednesday (2 minutes) • Teach and practice letter formation: handwriting with new letter from Wednesday (10–16 minutes)	• Phonological awareness warm-up (2–3 minutes) • Review activities: letter names and/or sounds on flashcards, high-frequency word flashcards if applicable, blending drill with support (2–3 minutes) • Optional: high-frequency word practice game (5–7 minutes) • Alphabet video and movement (2 minutes) • Sounds dictation on whiteboards (5–7 minutes) • Finish any remaining activities from the week, or play games (teacher discretion)

experience in a formal school setting. They might experience separa-tion anxiety from their families or struggle to get along with their peers. New kindergarteners also have a lot to learn about what it means to attend school. They need to learn your procedures, routines, and expec-tations (as well as the school rules), and spend ample time practicing them. Students need to feel safe in their learning environment so that they can successfully adjust and feel comfortable taking academic risks (which is essential to learning). Therefore, the first weeks and months of kindergarten should include significant amounts of time spent on teach-ing procedures, routines, and expectations, as well as building class-room community so students feel safe and welcomed at school. Rushing to begin small-group instruction means spending less time and focus on these important areas.

Additionally, the logistics involved in setting up small-group instruction make it difficult to begin immediately. When you work with a small group of students, the other students will need to be actively engaged in learning and/or play. Ideally, you want interruptions to your small group to be minimal. For this to happen, students need to learn how to safely complete activities on their own or with their peers. They also need to understand which materials should be used for each activity and how to take them out and store them appropriately. Even if your students are engaging in play rather than academic work, they need practice with social skills like turn-taking, sharing, and problem-solving. These skills take time to teach, and if you begin small-group instruction early on in the school year, you will not have sufficient time to support students in learning independent work and play skills. This leads to a greater likelihood that students will get off-task, engage in unsafe behaviors, or simply not understand what they are supposed to be working on. Time spent teaching procedures and routines at the beginning of the school year is time well spent. When you are ready to implement small-group instruction, students will have learned more independent work skills. By then, they will be less likely to interrupt your small groups, and more likely to spend their independent time in a productive manner.

That said, small-group instruction is an extremely valuable tool, and it's important to plan to incorporate it into your phonics instruction after those initial six to eight weeks of the school year. When you're ready to introduce small groups, assess students' alphabet knowledge (see the Appendix for tools to do so). Then, place them into groups based on the letters that they do and do not know. You will likely not have perfect match groups, but look for as much overlap as possible in terms of letters students do not yet know. Keep in mind that if you have not yet finished covering the entire alphabet in a whole-group setting by the time you introduce small groups, you will still want to continue with your whole-group phonics instruction until you have finished covering the rest of the letters.

Small-group instruction will help you target students' specific needs and spend time on the letters that they most need to learn—and eventually, read CVC (consonant-vowel-consonant) words and more challenging words. Small-group instruction will also help you ensure that students are paying attention, as well as make it easier to gather data on how students are progressing with their learning. In sum, small-group instruction is an important part of kindergarten phonics instruction. But again, I do not recommend fully implementing small groups at the beginning of the school year. If you can pull a few children for a quick small-group activity here and there during the first weeks and months of school, that's great. Just don't worry about dedicating a full block of time and seeing multiple small groups quite yet.

If you happen to have a co-teacher or highly trained classroom assistant who can lead the other students while you meet with small groups, you might be able to start small groups earlier on in the school year, compared to kindergarten teachers who do not have this level of support. Even then, I still recommend dedicating the first two to four weeks of school to teaching expectations and building classroom community.

How to Differentiate Your Alphabet Instruction

Although you will be teaching the letters to all your students, this does not mean that you can't differentiate! Many alphabet activities provide opportunities for students to develop multiple skills. You can also expand on alphabet activities to challenge your more advanced learners. In Table 7.2, you'll see a few suggestions for alphabet activities, the skills they can help students develop, and how you can use them to challenge your advanced students. This is, by no means, an exhaustive list of activities. Refer to Chapter 3 for complete kindergarten sample schedules for alphabet instruction that also includes explicit instruction on letter names, sounds, and formation, as well as explicit phonological awareness instruction.

In addition to the example challenges listed in Table 7.2, you can engage advanced students by making appropriate reading materials (usually decodable texts) available for them to access. You might choose a selection of books and place them in a basket for students to access when they finish a task early, or when you allow them to skip a task that will be far too easy for them.

Also consider how you can ask different types of questions throughout your phonics lessons (and literacy block as a whole) to engage students at a variety of levels. For example, if you're reading a big book to the entire class, you might ask questions like, "Where do I point to start reading?" or "Do you see any letters that you know?" or "Does anyone know what this word says?" Every question that you ask will not be just right for every learner, but by asking a range of questions and calling on the learners best-suited to answer those questions, you can provide challenges to all levels of students.

Table 7.2 Alphabet Activities and Ways to Differentiate Them

Activity	Learning Opportunities	Challenges to Offer
Students brainstorm words that begin with a target letter; teacher writes words on a board or chart paper.	Phonemic awareness (identifying words that begin with a target sound), learning speech to print connections, seeing the target letter in context	Students can write down their own list of words on a whiteboard or piece of paper, using invented spelling.
Teacher reads an alphabet rhyme or alliterative story to students (see Figure 7.1 for an example).	Phonemic awareness, print concepts (e.g., left-to-right tracking, concept of word), seeing the target letter in context	Students can follow along and read words as teacher reads them; teacher can occasionally pause to allow students to read a word independently if they are able to do so; readers can also be given a copy of the rhyme or book later on for independent rereading.
Students sort pictures, some that begin with the target letter sound and some that do not (see Figure 7.2 for an example).	Phonemic awareness, letter sound learning, vocabulary development	Students can use invented spelling (or prior spelling knowledge) to label each picture with a word; students can add additional words or pictures of their own to the sort; students can write sentences with the words.
Teacher dictates letter sounds for students to spell on whiteboards or in a sensory material.	Encoding skills, letter sound knowledge	Students can be invited to write the sound *and* a word that begins with the sound; teacher can also privately dictate CVC or other words to certain students.

138

FIGURE 7.1 Example alphabet rhyme.

What Comes After the Alphabet?

Following this model, you teach the alphabet to the class in a whole-group setting, assess students, and then begin small-group instruction. But what should you teach once students have mastered the alphabet?

As you might already know, the next step is learning to read vowel-consonant (VC) and consonant-vowel-consonant (CVC) words. However, this step should actually begin *before* students master the complete alphabet! As we have discussed in previous chapters, research shows us that students best learn phonics skills when they have opportunities to *apply* them. This is true for learning the alphabet, too! Students need supported opportunities to read and spell words as they are learning the letters. This means that we do not want to wait until we finish covering the alphabet (or until students master the alphabet) and then suddenly ask students to begin reading and spelling words. Instead, we should provide supported practice opportunities with VC and CVC words as part of our alphabet instruction.

As soon as students know a handful of letters, you can begin modeling the blending drill (discussed in detail in Chapter 2), using only the letters that students have been taught. For example, if students have

FIGURE 7.2 Example picture sort.

FIGURE 7.3 Blending drill with a VC word.

learned the letters *a* and *t*, you can model blending to read the word *at* (see Figure 7.3). Here is how you can provide support to your students (note that the teacher would point underneath each letter card individually when saying each sound, and then sweep her finger underneath the letter cards to model blending):

Teacher: I'm going to say each letter sound and blend them to read the whole word. Show me a thumbs-up if you're ready! My turn: /ă/ /t/, *at*. Now let's do it together.

Teacher and students: /ă/ /t/, *at*. (Teacher points.)

Teacher: Now it's your turn.

Students: /ă/ /t/, *at*. (Teacher points.)

Teacher: Good job! What word did you read?

Students: *At*.

Teacher: Yes! We are *at* school today.

This example uses a VC word, but you can also model how to read CVC words. You might only get through one to two words at first, but you can gradually increase the number of words per practice session as students learn more letters. As we discussed in Chapter 3, blending will be easier for students when you use words that begin with the continuous sounds for the letters *a, e, f, i, l, m, n, o, r, s, u, v, w, y*, and *z*. An example of a word that begins with a continuous sound is *mat*. An example of a word that begins with a stop sound, however, is *dip*.

Ultimately, the goal is for students to blend to read words on their own. By incorporating just a few minutes of practice most days of the week while you are still teaching the alphabet, students will begin to see how letters are used to make words (the alphabetic principle), practice letter sounds, and practice blending. It will also help the transition from letters to reading go much more smoothly for many children.

Additionally, children should have supported experiences with using their letter-sound knowledge to spell words. This can happen during writing time when you encourage students to express their ideas using invented spelling. However, this should also happen in a more structured setting, when you guide students in spelling VC and CVC words. Just like with the blending drill, only choose words with letters that students have been taught.

At first, students will need a great deal of support to spell words. Your work together might sound something like this:

Teacher: Let's spell some words with the vowel we just learned, short *e*. Please take out your magnetic letters. (Students each take out a magnetic board with magnetic tiles for each letter.)

Teacher: Our first word is *pet*. I like to pet my dog. Say *pet*.

Students: *Pet*.

Teacher: The sounds in *pet* are /p//ĕ//t/. (If students can successfully segment the word, have them do it on their own, or along with you.) Say /p//ĕ//t/.

Students: /p//ĕ//t/.

Teacher: What is the first sound you hear?

Students: /p/ (If students do not know, simply tell them the sound.)

Teacher: What letter says /p/?

Students: p

Teacher: Find the letter p to start your word. (Waits for students to locate the letter and bring it down to start building a word.)

Teacher: /p//ĕ//t/. We spelled the /p/ . . . what comes next?

Students: /ĕ/ (If students do not know, simply tell them the sound.)

Teacher: What letter should we use to spell /ĕ/?

Students: e

Teacher: Yes! Add the letter e after your p. (Waits for students to locate the letter and bring it down to continue building the word.)

Teacher: Now we have /p//ĕ/, pĕ . . . what sound comes at the end of pet?

Students: /t/ (If students do not know, simply tell them the sound.)

Teacher: Yes, the last sound is /t/! What letter should we use to spell /t/?

Students: t

Teacher: Yes! Add the letter t to finish your word. (Waits for students to locate the letter and bring it down to continue building the word.)

Teacher: Put your finger under the letter p. We are going to say each sound and blend to read the word, like this: /p//ĕ/, pe, /t/, pet. Let's do it together.

Teacher and Students: /p//ĕ/, pe, /t/, pet (while pointing).

Teacher: What word did you spell?

Students: *Pet*!

Teacher: Great job! To pet something can mean to touch it gently, like if you use your hand to pet a hamster. A pet can also be an animal that people take care of, like a dog or a cat or a bird. Put your letters back; let's try one more word.

Just like with the blending drill, this process will take a long time at first. Eventually, you want students to be able to segment and spell a word without needing modeling and letter-by-letter support. However, it will take time and practice to get to this point. At first, you might even find that you need to give more support than what is described in the scenario.

Post-Alphabet Small-Group Instruction

Although you will give all students supportive practice with reading and spelling VC and CVC words as they are learning the alphabet, kindergarten students vary in terms of when they are ready to complete these tasks with more independence, as well as to read entire sentences and decodable texts. This is why small-group instruction comes in handy. Once you have finished teaching the alphabet in a whole-group setting, as described previously, you can begin meeting with small groups. Some small groups might still be working on letters, and others will be ready to move on to CVC words (or beyond). Because children develop at different rates, small-group instruction will enable you to meet your students where they are at.

In Chapter 3, you learned about whole-class instruction with built-in differentiation. Although you might be able to incorporate certain elements of this chapter into your instruction and complete some activities in a whole-group setting (e.g., high-frequency word instruction, the blending drill), I do not recommend that 100% of your phonics and reading instruction take place in a whole-group setting for kindergarten students. At this age, it's easier for students to pay attention and learn when they are given direct teacher support, as compared to when they are expected to follow along with the entire group. Whole-group instruction is absolutely valuable for kindergarten (and all) students, but if at all possible, I recommend reserving a significant portion of your phonics instruction for the small-group setting (after you finish alphabet instruction). You can refer to Table 4.1 in Chapter 4 for more details on what activities you might choose for your small groups.

References

Justice, L. M., Pence, K. L., Bowles, R. P., & Wiggins, A. (2006). An investigation of four hypotheses concerning the order by which 4-year-old children learn the alphabet letters. *Early Childhood Research Quarterly, 21*(3), 374–389. https://doi.org/10.1016/j.ecresq.2006.07.010

McBride-Chang, C. (1999). The ABCs of the ABCS: The development of letter-name and letter-sound knowledge. *Merrill-Palmer Quarterly, 45*(2), 285–308. https://digitalcommons.wayne.edu/cgi/viewcontent.cgi?article=1032&context=mpq

Mesmer, H. A. (2019). *Letter lessons and first words: Phonics foundations that work.* Heinemann Educational Books.

Piasta, S. B., & Wagner, R. K. (2010). Developing early literacy skills: A meta-analysis of alphabet learning and instruction. *Reading Research Quarterly, 45*(1), 8–38. https://doi.org/10.1598/RRQ.45.1.2

Stahl, Katherine A. Dougherty. (2014). New insights about letter learning. *The Reading Teacher, 68*(4), 261–265. https://doi.org/10.1002/trtr.1320

Considerations for English Language Learners

I will never forget my first experience working with a student who spoke little English, while also teaching an entire class of students. At the time, I was student teaching in the second grade, and I had a relatively diverse class of students. This group of children was culturally and ethnically diverse, but not linguistically diverse. All of the kids in my class had been speaking English since they were very young.

Then, toward the end of my student teaching experience, a new student arrived. His family had come directly from Mexico, and he spoke no English. "No problem," I thought to myself. I spoke Spanish and had tutored many students (one-on-one or in small groups) who were learning English as a second language. I was excited to get to know our new student.

Very quickly, however, I realized that supporting this student was not going to be as easy as I had originally thought. Although I could communicate with him, and although I had experience working with English language learners in small-group settings, I had never experienced a situation in which I was teaching an entire class of children and one student could not understand anything that I was saying. I had no idea where to begin, and I felt somewhat powerless to help him. Luckily for me (and for him), he soon began receiving plenty of pull-out English support. My student teaching commitment was also wrapping up, so I didn't end up spending a great deal of time working with him.

This experience opened my eyes to the challenges of working with a large group of children and simultaneously supporting those students who are learning English as a second (or third or fourth!) language. I wanted to better understand how I could help individual students while still teaching an entire class. In pursuit of this goal, I ultimately went on to earn endorsements in teaching English to language learners.

If you are working with multilingual language learners, it's easy to focus on students' "deficits," or what they do not know. However, these learners (like any children) already possess valuable linguistic and cultural knowledge, even if it is different from our own or from that of other students. Multilingual learners are certainly not starting at zero. Our job as teachers is to build on their existing knowledge and help them add English to their repertoires, not replace the other language(s) that they speak. We also need to employ the right tools and strategies to ensure that our multilingual learners are successful.

How to Teach Phonics to Multilingual Language Learners

Multilingual language learners benefit from explicit, systematic phonics instruction. Sound familiar? You might recall from Chapter 2 that *all* students benefit from explicit, systematic phonics instruction! This is great news, because it means that we can teach phonics to our multilingual language learners through the same overall approach that we use to teach phonics to all our students.

That said, we still need to use scaffolds, or supports, to ensure that our multilingual language learners master the *content of phonics* (the skills found in our scope and sequence) and the *language of phonics* (vocabulary terms like *vowel* or *syllable*). In this chapter, we'll discuss a variety of supports that you can use to help students master both areas, as well as build additional vocabulary knowledge during phonics instruction. Because you are already working with words as you teach phonics (*banana* for the letter *Bb*, for example, or *unhappy* when you are teaching prefixes), this instructional time can be leveraged to grow students' overall vocabularies.

The supports in this chapter can be used in whole-group and small-group settings. Working with multilingual language learners in a small-group setting can, in fact, be a scaffold in itself. In a small-group setting, you can provide more opportunities for students to speak and build language. It's often easier to observe individual students' progress toward learning the skills and concepts you're teaching. A small-group setting can also make it easier to adjust the pace or content of your instruction to meet students' needs (e.g., spending more time teaching vocabulary terms). Just keep in mind that, although small groups can be highly beneficial, you can still meet multilingual learners' needs in whole-group instruction, as long as you provide the right supports.

Getting to Know Your Students

Before we begin to explore specific strategies and scaffolds, we need to make sure that we understand our students' needs. Just like any group of students, multilingual language learners all have unique strengths and areas for growth. Some students might be highly proficient in English, whereas others are still learning their first words in English. Some multilingual learners might have outstanding phonics knowledge, while others are still working to accurately hear and pronounce the sounds of English.

In Chapter 1, we discussed the value of assessment data in delivering effective phonics instruction. When working with multilingual learners, you'll want to obtain data about their phonics knowledge, but you'll also want to seek out data about their current levels of English knowledge.

You can certainly observe students' English skills anecdotally as you speak and work with them in your classroom. However, research indicates that most multilingual learners display social proficiency in English before they have achieved a high level of proficiency in academic English (Thomas & Collier, 1997). In other words, students might appear to know more English than they actually do. This is why it's important to seek out information about their levels of language knowledge.

Your school might give multilingual learners a yearly proficiency test in English. You can review the results (and consult with any ESL specialists in your building) to learn what your multilingual learners can do proficiently, and what they are still working on. If this type of data is not available to you, ask your school or district ESL specialists if they have any informal test results that you can review. Pay special attention to differences in your students' *receptive* and *expressive* language skills. Receptive language skills enable students to understand spoken and written language. Expressive language skills enable students to speak and write. The receptive skill of understanding spoken language usually comes before the expressive skill of speaking. This means that a multilingual learner might understand more of your instruction than what they can express verbally. The receptive skill of reading also comes before the expressive skill of writing. Writing can be particularly challenging for multilingual learners.

Understanding how your students are progressing in their receptive and expressive language skills helps you make accommodations in your instruction and assessment. For example, if you know that a student's expressive language skills make it difficult for them to respond in complete sentences, you might provide a sentence starter to help get them started (more on this later). If you do not have any data on your multilingual learners' English language abilities, simply being aware of the differences between receptive and expressive language can help you gauge how students are doing and tailor your instruction accordingly. The better you know your students, the easier it will be to choose the right scaffolds so that they can be successful.

Scaffolds That Support Receptive Language Skills

Let's begin with some different tools and strategies you can use to help your multilingual learners understand spoken and written language during your phonics lessons. Note that even though we are focusing on receptive language, some of these strategies will also support expressive language skills! (Who doesn't love a two-for-one?)

Use Pared Down Language

When you are teaching a phonics lesson (or any lesson, for that matter), you'll want to pay attention to your own use of oral language. Multilingual learners benefit when we use simplified, or pared-down, language to teach a concept or give instructions. This does not mean that we do not use age-appropriate vocabulary words. It simply means that we pay attention to how many words we use when we communicate, how specific and clear those words are, and how we explain words that are unfamiliar to our learners.

To further understand the concept of pared-down language, let's look at how two different teachers might explain the same task during a phonics lesson. Ask yourself, "Which teacher's explanation would be easier for multilingual learners—or any learners—to understand?"

Teacher A: Now you're going to read a list of words with vowel teams *AI* and *AY*. Remember what those vowel teams say? Right, the long *a* sound, /ā/. (Writes both vowel teams on the board.) Before you read the list, you need to use your highlighter to highlight *AI* and *AY*. You don't need to color the whole word, just the *AI* or *AY*. It shouldn't take that long. (Teacher models doing this for one of the words on the list.) After you highlight, read the word to yourself . . . and then, um, let's also have you read the word list to your phonics partner. Okay?

Teacher B: The vowel teams *AI* and AY can represent the long *a* sound, /ā/. (Writes both vowel teams on the board.) I'll give you a list of words. First, highlight the letters *AI* or *AY* in each word. (Teacher models doing this for one of the words on the list.) Second, read the words to yourself. Third, read the list to your phonics partner.

Both teachers' explanations are acceptable, and both teachers included modeling (showing students how to highlight a vowel team) to support their spoken directions. However, you probably noticed that Teacher B's language was clearer and more concise. It included fewer extra words and phrases like "um" or "let's also have you." Teacher B's sentences were shorter. She also used the words *first*, *second*, and *third* to give clear action steps. For these reasons, it would be easier for multilingual language learners to comprehend Teacher B's explanation, when compared to Teacher A's explanation.

In the hectic pace of our school days, it can be difficult to pay attention to our own language use. A simple strategy you can try is to record yourself during a lesson or two. Listen back and ask yourself if your language sounded more like that of Teacher A or that of Teacher B. No human being is going to use language perfectly every single moment of the day, but perhaps you can find opportunities where you can pare down and simplify your teacher talk. This will ultimately benefit all your students, not just your multilingual language learners.

Use Modeling, Pictures, and Other Visual Aids

Verbal explanations during your phonics lessons are important, but they should be supported by visual input. As you saw in the examples with Teacher A and Teacher B, teacher modeling can provide important visual input to help students understand directions. Teacher modeling is an important part of explicit instruction, and it should also be used when teaching specific skills and concepts to students. Here is an example of

how a teacher uses modeling to demonstrate to students how to decode
words with the inflectional ending -*ing*.

Teacher: Now you know that the -*ing* chunk can say /*ing*/. Let's
practice reading words with the -*ing* ending. (Writes *fixing*
on the board, so all students can see it.)

If you know the word, don't shout it out! Watch what I do.
(Uses her hand to cover up the -*ing* ending.) First, I read the
word without the ending. We can call this the base word.
(Circles *fix* with her finger, then underneath each letter individually as she sounds it out.) /*f*/ /*ĭ*/ /*ks*/, *fix*. The base
word says *fix*. Now, I uncover the word ending. (Uncovers
the -*ing* ending) I already know this says /*ing*/. So I put the
two parts together: *fix-ing*. The word is *fixing*. I am fixing
my bike so I can ride it again.

After this example, the teacher models again with the word
dusting. This time, however, she invites students to decode
the word *dust* and put the two word parts together to
read *dusting*. Last, the teacher finds an example of a word
with *ing* in a book she recently read aloud to the class. She
enlarges the text using a document camera and leads the
class in decoding this word using the same strategy.

Notice how this teacher wrote the word *fixing* on the board so that
all students could see it, used her hand to show students how to cover
up the ending, and pointed to each letter as she said its sound. She
explained what she was doing, step-by-step, to provide verbal input as
well as visual input from her physical demonstration. By having students practice this strategy in a real text, she illustrated when they can
use this strategy (as they are reading).

It's likely that modeling is already an important part of your teaching practice. When you're considering how to best teach your multilingual language learners, keep in mind that a little extra modeling might

be needed. For example, although some students might remember how to complete an activity that they've done previously, your multilingual language learners might not know what to do if you simply provide a verbal explanation or reminder. Taking the time to remodel will give them the support they need to be successful. Again, all your students will benefit from extra attention to modeling!

Teacher modeling is, of course, not the only way to provide visual input to support your phonics lessons. Images (photos, clipart, etc.) can reinforce concepts that you also explain verbally. Images are helpful for all students, not just multilingual language learners. However, you'll need to be thoughtful and intentional about incorporating images into your phonics instruction. When we are teaching phonics, we want to focus students' attention primarily on the print, so they learn the relationships between letters and sounds. We don't want to give students a word to decode and then also provide a picture of the word, because many students will simply guess the word from the picture, rather than attend to the letter-sound relationships. Similarly, before we give our students a decodable text to read, we need to evaluate the book and make sure that students will not be able to guess many (or any) of the words by looking at the pictures. At times, texts organized as passages (see Figure 8.1, an example from *From Sounds to Spelling*) rather than books can be especially helpful, because passages typically contain fewer images that students can potentially use for guessing words.

So, then, when *should* we use images during our phonics instruction? Here are a few examples of when images can be helpful:

- **Picture sorts:** These are used for phonological awareness development, rather than phonics, but they also support students' phonics learning. For example, you might give students a sort where they put pictures into two groups based on their vowel sound.

- **Key words or example words for a specific phonics pattern:** For example, a picture of a tree on a poster for the vowel team *ee*, like in Figure 8.2. You might display visual aids like this poster in your classroom or work space so that students can refer back to them.

Name:	Skill: Ending s-blends	Words to Pre-teach: help, trike

The Chest

Rod sat at his desk with the big chest. It had a lock with rust on

it. To get the lock off the chest was his quest.

Dad was in bed. He had to rest. Rod did not ask for his help.

"First, I will hit the lock with a brush."

That cost Rod his brush.

"I will ram the chest with my trike!"

Rod took a risk and went fast.

Now Rod has no trike. And the lock is still on the chest!

Circle all of the words in the text that end with -sk or -st.

What did Rod do to try to open the chest?

FIGURE 8.1 Example of a decodable passage.

- **Words that you choose to spend a little extra time on for vocabulary development:** For example, the vocabulary poster in Figure 8.3 shows a word taught when students are working on the *ier* pattern.
- **Spelling activities in which students name a picture and spell the word:** See Figure 8.4 for an example. One caution here is that you must pre-teach the names of the pictures if students do not already know them.

FIGURE 8.2 Keyword phonics poster for *ee* vowel team.

FIGURE 8.3 Example vocabulary poster.

Spelling Long I CVCe Words

Say the name of the picture out loud. Spell the word.
Silent e at the end has an "open box" because the e does not make a sound.

| p | i | n | e |

5 [ ][ ][ ]

[ ][ ][ ]

q [ ][ ][ ]

h [ ][ ]

[ ][ ][ ][ ]

Write a sentence with at least one of the words.

_____

- -

_____

- -

©2020 From Sounds to Spelling, Level 1 Week 24

FIGURE 8.4 Spelling activity.

In sum, choose images that support your phonics instruction and students' learning of related vocabulary words, but be careful that they do not detract from the phonics learning tasks at hand.

Just like images, videos can also be a powerful tool to support students' language comprehension. Here are a few examples of the types of videos you might occasionally incorporate into your phonics lessons:

- Teaching videos that explain a phonics concept to students

- Short informational clips that explain more about the topic of a decodable text (e.g., a video showing how a crane is used in construction when you have students read a decodable text about cranes)

- Short informational clips that help explain the meaning of a word you are focusing on

Modeling, images, and videos can help you show, not just tell, as you teach phonics to your multilingual language learners and all your students.

Explicitly Define Key Vocabulary Terms

During your phonics lessons, there are two main types of vocabulary words that you'll want to teach: the words that students are learning to read and spell and terms that make up the language of phonics.

Let's first consider the words that students are learning. Our goal is for students to be able to spell and read many words. When students also understand the meaning of a word, they have acquired more complete knowledge of the word. It's more likely that this word will stick, that students will retain it in the future. To accomplish this, we want to help students activate three parts in their brains when learning a new word: where the spelling of a word is stored, where the sounds in the word are stored, and where the meaning of the word is stored (Blevins, 2016). This is true for all students, not just multilingual language learners. Therefore, we would be remiss if we did not incorporate vocabulary development into our phonics instruction with all of our students.

You might wonder how to incorporate vocabulary instruction while still maintaining students' focus on the phonics skill(s) you're teaching in a lesson. First, you might choose a few words (two to four) per week to spend more time on for vocabulary development, as we do in *From Sounds to Spelling*. Second, make it a habit to provide a quick definition or example for some of the other words students are reading or spelling. Here are some examples of practices to incorporate:

- Each time you dictate a word for students to build or write, make sure to use the word in a sentence.
- After students read a list of words, choose a few to define and/or ask students questions about.
- If you're teaching the alphabet, show students pictures of many words that begin with each letter.

When you define a word, do not have students guess the meaning. Simply provide a quick explanation and move on (Beck et al., 2013). At times, you might want to have a picture ready to further illustrate the meaning of the word. Prepare ahead of time by searching the internet for relevant picture(s) and placing them in a word processing document to easily pull up for students. Teachers who work with multilingual language learners should remember to define at least some terms that are common, or that many other students know, rather than assuming that their multilingual language learners already know these words. If you are working with multilingual language learners in a small-group setting, you might have students read and spell fewer words overall so that you can spend a bit more time on vocabulary development. For example, instead of having students read a list of 10 words, you might have them read 7 or 8.

Keep in mind that whether you are working with multilingual language learners or not, your goal is to *quickly* acquaint students with the meanings of many words you are working on. You will not be able to spend time discussing the meaning of every single word students encounter during a phonics lesson. Additional, in-depth vocabulary instruction should take place at another point in your school day.

Next, let's discuss the terms that make up the language of phonics. These are words like *consonant, digraph, blend, vowel team, diphthong,* and *syllable* that can help students understand and discuss the phonics concepts you're teaching. These words can be especially challenging for multilingual language learners because they are somewhat abstract. They cannot be represented by an image. However, you can provide a definition and examples. The first time you teach students about a vowel team, make sure to define the term *vowel team* (a group of vowels working together, often to represent a long vowel sound). You might write this definition on a piece of chart paper and include a few examples. As you teach students more vowel teams, add to the list of examples. Make sure to review the definitions of these terms often to ensure that multilingual language learners (and all students) understand your instruction during phonics lessons.

Break Up Decodable Texts into Chunks

So far, we have discussed how to support students' receptive language during our instruction, as we give directions and as we have students read and spell individual words. However, we also need to create scaffolds for multilingual language learners as they read entire texts. As we discussed in Chapter 2, a decodable text is a story, passage, or other text in which the words are restricted to include only phonics patterns and high-frequency words that students have already been taught. They are an excellent tool for giving students in-context phonics practice.

However, decodable texts can be particularly tricky for multilingual language learners to comprehend. Because decodable texts seek to give students practice with specific types of words, they sometimes contain a greater quantity of unusual words or words that are new to students. For example, students might encounter the word *fig* or *dim* in a text that focuses on short *i*. Decodable texts, like any texts, might also contain language structures that differ from the everyday conversational language to which students are accustomed. Sometimes the sentence structure in decodable texts can even feel stilted because authors are restricted by the types of words that they can include. All of these elements can pose challenges for multilingual language learners' comprehension.

Although the purpose of a decodable text is primarily to have students practice applying their phonics skills to decode, we also want children to understand the texts that they're reading. We don't want to inadvertently teach them that reading is only about sounding out the words, not making meaning from the text. As we discussed in previous sections, defining at least some tricky vocabulary words supports multilingual language learners' comprehension. Another helpful strategy is to break up decodable texts into smaller chunks (two, three, or four, depending on the length of the text). After each chunk, pause and ask students to retell what the author has said in the text so far. You might even have students self-evaluate their own comprehension by giving a thumbs-up or thumbs-to-the-side hand signal. You can then decide if you can have students keep reading or if you want to stop and provide additional explanations.

For example, if you have students begin reading a decodable passage for vowel team *ea* on the topic of dreams and you discover, two paragraphs in, that students do not know what the word *dream* means, then you can stop and provide an explanation. Without that explanation, the entire text would not make much sense to students so that check-in serves as an important scaffold. Or perhaps your students do understand what the words mean, but they are struggling with comprehending the sentences. In this case, you might break down a few important sentences to discuss with students before allowing them to continue reading.

As you might imagine, using more frequent checkpoints takes up more time. However, this is time well spent, because multilingual language learners need to acquire receptive language skills just as much as they need to learn phonics. Working with students in a small-group setting can be helpful in implementing this strategy because some groups might need multiple checkpoints and other groups might be able to read through the entire text independently.

One final note on working with multilingual language learners in decodable texts: be careful not to give away too much to students. You want the text to be a little bit challenging for students, in terms of the phonics content, vocabulary, and language structures. If the text is easy (or you make the text too easy by providing extensive scaffolding), then there is no productive struggle or space for students to learn from the text. Avoid lengthy book introductions that give away most of the plot points or words. Allow students to make mistakes and have time to think before you dive in and help. Just like all our students, multilingual language learners need challenges in order to grow.

Recap: Receptive Language Strategies for Multilingual Language Learners

To summarize, here are the strategies we covered that can support students' language comprehension during phonics lessons:

- Use pared-down language.
- Use modeling, pictures, and other visual aids.
- Explicitly define vocabulary (words students are learning and words that make up the language of phonics).
- Break up decodable texts into smaller chunks for discussion.

Remember, these strategies benefit all learners, not just your multilingual language learners.

Scaffolds That Support Expressive Language Skills

Next, let's explore tools and strategies you can use to help your multilingual learners speak and write during your phonics lessons. These strategies can also be helpful for supporting receptive language skills, as well as with students who are not multilingual language learners.

Teach Students to Attend to Mouth Position When Forming Sounds

For students to learn phonics, they must make connections between letters and their sounds. If students are not pronouncing sounds correctly, this can interfere with their reading and spelling. Some children experience delays or challenges with articulation, pronouncing speech sounds. Multilingual language learners might also have trouble pronouncing speech sounds that do not appear in the other languages they speak. For example, a child who speaks Spanish might struggle with the sound for digraph *sh* in English, because this sound does not exist in the Spanish language.

To help students pronounce sounds correctly for the purposes of word reading, research (e.g., Roberts et al., 2019) indicates that specific articulation instruction can be beneficial. Help students pay attention to how their mouths (including lips, tongue, and teeth) are positioned when a sound is pronounced. Show students your mouth, and provide small mirrors so that students can see their own mouths when practicing. You might follow this sequence when describing a speech sound to students:

1. Say the sound, and have students attempt to repeat it.

2. Direct students to look at your mouth, and say the sound again.

3. Explain how your mouth is positioned to form the sound.

4. Give students mouth position directions and have them say the sound.

5. Have students practice a few times, preferably with small mirrors. Provide corrective feedback.

Here's an example of what this might sound like:

Teacher: Let's practice the sound /f/. Try to say /f/.

Students: /f/. (Some make mistakes.)

Teacher: Look at my mouth while I say it. /f/.

Teacher: To make the /f/ sound, I touch my top teeth to my bottom lip, like this. Then, I blow air. /f/.

Teacher: Your turn! Put your teeth on top of your bottom lip. (Pause.) Now blow a little air.

Students: /f/.

Students continue to practice with mirrors while the teacher corrects students and reinforces correct mouth positioning as needed. If you're not quite sure how to describe the mouth position of a sound, explanations can easily be found by searching online.

This sequence can be done in a whole-group setting, but it is often easier to provide corrective feedback when working with students in a small group. You might need to repeat the suggested sequence multiple times before a student can pronounce the sound. Something to keep in mind is that many multilingual language learners never learn to pronounce certain English-specific speech sounds traditionally, though they can still read, write, and understand words with those sounds. This is not problematic. However, if you're not sure if a student is struggling to pronounce a sound due to the influence of other language(s) they speak or due to a speech delay, ask your school's speech and language pathologist for input.

Provide Sentence Starters

Sentence starters, or sentence frames, are helpful tools that can support students in their speaking and writing. A sentence starter gives students part of a sentence, and they are asked to fill in the rest (e.g., the words *I would go to* in Figure 8.5). They help teach language structure and make it easier for students to express their thoughts in complete sentences.

You might use sentence starters when you ask students to answer a question with a partner. For example, if you ask, "How many vowels are in the word *helpful*?", you might write on the board and read to students, "There are ___ vowels in the word _____" to help them answer the question. Or, if students are writing about a decodable text that they read, you might get them started by writing this sentence starter on the board: "This story took place in _____."

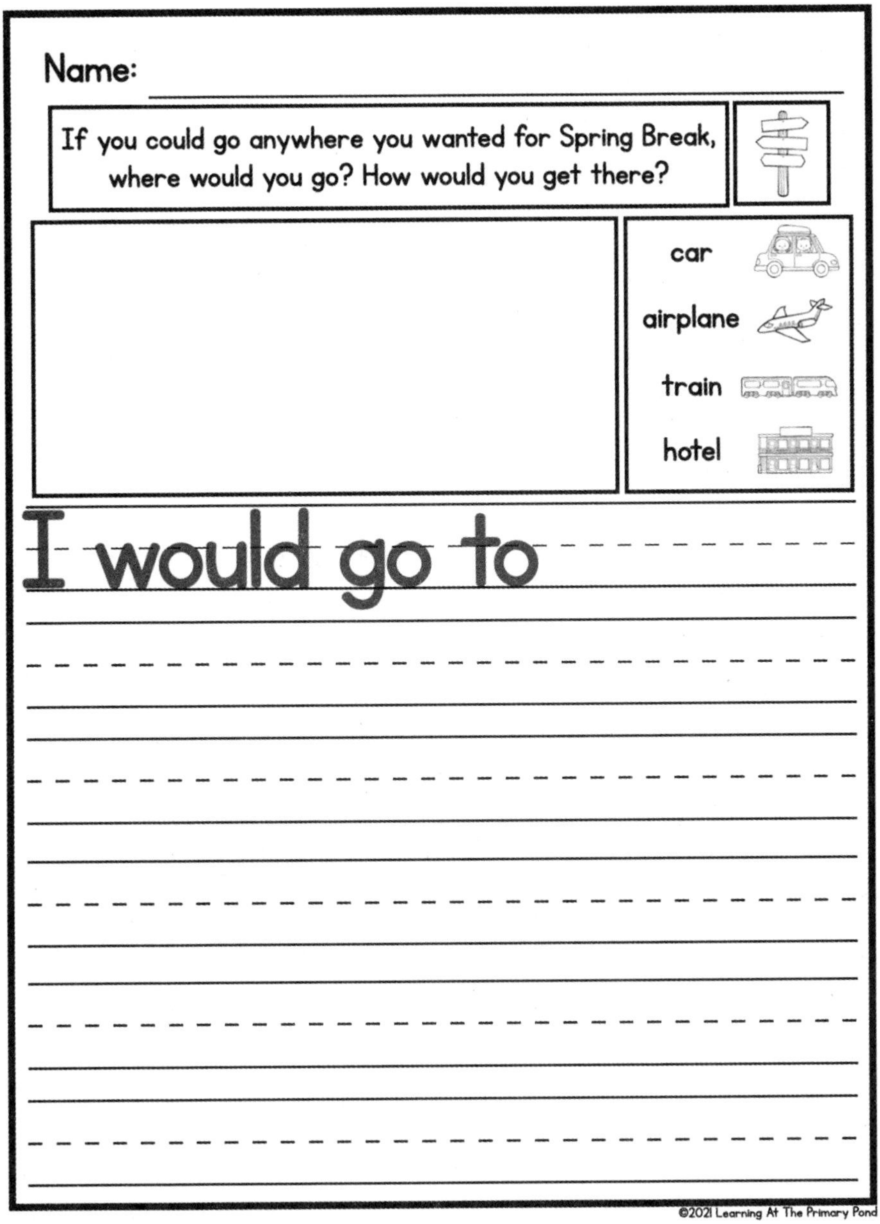

Name: _____

If you could go anywhere you wanted for Spring Break, where would you go? How would you get there?

car

airplane

train

hotel

I would go to _____

_____

_____

_____

_____

_____

_____

_____

©2021 Learning At The Primary Pond

FIGURE 8.5 Sentence starter example.

When you dictate a sentence for students to write, you typically will not want to provide students with a sentence starter (unless students are just beginning to write words for the first time and cannot write an entire sentence). To review, dictation is an instructional activity in which students practice applying their phonics and high-frequency word knowledge to writing a sentence that you construct. Multilingual language learners might need to hear you repeat the sentence a greater number of times than other students do. They are not as familiar yet with the structures of English, and this can make it harder for them to recall the sentence as they are writing it. All students, however, should have the opportunity to hear you say the sentence and to repeat the sentence with you before they are asked to write the sentence.

Create Frequent Opportunities for Oral Language Practice

Students benefit from opportunities to practice oral language skills (by talking) throughout the school day. You might think, "Of course, kids are going to talk at school!" Although that's certainly true, we need to intentionally plan for those opportunities, especially when we're working with multilingual language learners.

In a traditional classroom environment, the teacher asks a question, students raise their hands, and one or two students respond when they are called on. This pattern is repeated throughout the school day. There is nothing wrong with asking a question and having students raise their hands to respond, but if this is the primary way that you ask your students questions, students are missing out on valuable talk time. During your phonics lessons (or when teaching any subject), plan out some turn-and-talks ahead of time. In a turn-and-talk (sometimes also called *think-pair-share* or *partner talk*), students listen to a question, have a moment to think about their answer, and then turn to a student sitting near them to respond. The teacher typically still calls on a pair of students to share their answers once students have finished speaking to each other. Turn-and-talks allow all students to respond to a question (great for their academic development) and practice oral language skills.

When compared to certain activities like a read-aloud, your phonics lessons might not naturally contain quite as many opportunities for turn-and-talks. However, here are some examples of when you might incorporate them:

- When asking students to name words that start with or contain a certain sound

- When having students identify which letters make up the digraph in a word

- When asking students to come up with a sentence that contains a target high-frequency word or vocabulary word

It can be helpful to make a note in your lesson plans to indicate which questions you plan to ask as turn-and-talks.

Turn-and-talks provide an excellent opportunity for students to use oral language skills, but there are other ways to get students talking, too. For example, when you're reading a decodable text with students (preferably in a small-group setting), introduce the topic and ask students what they already know about it before they read. After students read the text, have them lead the retelling as much as possible. Partner practice activities can also provide opportunities for conversation. Students might work together on a game, word sort, or other activity. Some of the conversation will focus on the pragmatics of how to complete the activity, and there might be some level of off-topic conversation, but that is to be expected with young students (and human beings in general!). Regardless, these are still excellent opportunities for multilingual language learners to improve their oral language skills. To ensure that talk time is productive, here are some tips:

- Model productive, on-task conversations with another teacher or a volunteer student. Model unproductive conversations, too, and teach students how to get a conversation back on track.

- Provide sentence starters to help students structure their responses. Even just saying, "You can start by saying, 'I think that ____'" can help get them going.

- Consider specifying which student in each pair will speak first. For example, you assign half of your students to be peanut butter and the other half are jelly, and you tell students if peanut butter or jelly should speak first. I have also passed out two colors of rubber bracelets for students to wear (blue bracelets match up with orange bracelets, and orange speaks first). This way, you can ensure that one child is not doing all of the talking.

- Teach students how to respond to each other's responses. You might teach them sentence starters like "I agree that _____" or "I disagree. I think that _____" or "I also think that _____."

Partner Students Strategically

Once in a while, you might want to allow students to choose whom they work with for turn-and-talks or partner activities. However, it can be very helpful to assign consistent partners for students to work with for a month or quarter. Students' comfort level with and willingness to take academic risks might increase when they are accustomed to working with the same person. With time, a pair of students might also learn how to work together more effectively. Students don't have to work with the same partner all day, however. You might assign students one partner for phonics, reading, and social studies, and a different partner for math and science. Or, you might assign students one partner for when they are sitting on the rug for a lesson, and another partner for centers.

All students benefit when you strategically assign partners, multilingual language learners or not. For example, you might have a student who is working on below-level phonics skills partner up with a student working on grade level. The below-level student can learn from their partner. Plus, teaching a topic is one of the best ways to synthesize learning, so the more proficient peer can also strengthen their knowledge of a concept. When you give some thought to assigning partnerships, you can also consider which students get along well with each other in order to make the partnerships productive.

When multilingual language learners have the opportunity to work with a peer who is more advanced in English, their peer can serve as a language model for them. Without any effort on their part, their peer might expose them to new vocabulary words or reinforce the meanings of words and support them with sentence structure, simply by speaking to and with them.

Recap: Expressive Language Strategies for Multilingual Language Learners

Here are the strategies we covered that can support students' use of oral and written language during phonics lessons:

- Teach students to pay attention to their mouth positioning when pronouncing sounds.
- Provide sentence starters.
- Create frequent opportunities for oral language practice.
- Partner students strategically so that multilingual learners have a language model.

Once again, these strategies benefit all students, not just multilingual language learners.

Removing Scaffolds

Gaining academic proficiency in English takes most multilingual language learners four to seven years (Thomas & Collier, 1997). Therefore, although you should see some progress in your students' language acquisition, it's important to keep in mind that this will take time.

Many of the scaffolds you'll use for your multilingual language learners and all students are best practices that should be continued throughout the year (e.g., frequent opportunities for oral language practice, strategic partnering of students, using pared-down language, modeling, using visual aids, explicitly defining vocabulary). However, it's also important to consider removing scaffolds, when appropriate. For example, perhaps you begin mixing in some opportunities for turn-and-talks when you do not provide students with a sentence starter to get going. Or, maybe you notice that a group of multilingual language learners is doing well with their comprehension of decodable texts, so you remove the checkpoint that you usually include as they read the text.

There are no hard-and-fast rules about when to remove scaffolds. The best thing you can do for your students is to challenge them at times. Sometimes they will surprise you! Plus, if you remove a scaffold and discover that students still need it, there's no harm in reinstating it.

Viewing All Students as Language Learners

As we've discussed many times throughout this chapter, the strategies that benefit multilingual language learners also benefit all students. All of our students, especially in grades kindergarten through third, are language learners! They are learning vocabulary, sentence structure and grammar, oral expression, reading, and written expression. Therefore, whether or not you work with multilingual language learners, it's important to consider and plan for how you will help your students acquire all kinds of language.

References

Beck, I. L., McKeown, M. G., & Kucan, L. (2013). *Bringing words to life robust vocabulary instruction*. Guilford Press.

Blevins, W. (2016). *A fresh look at phonics, grades K–2: Common causes of failure and 7 ingredients for success*. Corwin Press.

Roberts, T. A., Vadasy, P. F., & Sanders, E. A. (2019). Preschoolers' alphabet learning: Cognitive, teaching sequence, and English proficiency influences. *Reading Research Quarterly*, 54(3), 413–437. doi:10.1002/rrq.242

Thomas, Wayne, P., & Collier, Virginia. (1997). School effectiveness for language minority students. NCBE Resource Collection Series, No. 9. https://eric.ed.gov/?id=ED436087

CHAPTER NINE

How to Differentiate Students' Independent Phonics Practice Activities

Throughout this book, we've discussed how to differentiate phonics activities that are largely *teacher-directed*. In Chapter 4, we touched briefly on what the other students are working on while you work with small groups. In this chapter, we're going to dive deeper into how you can differentiate students' independent phonics practice tasks. These activities might take place during your phonics block, literacy centers, or any other type of independent work structure that you use in your classroom.

Differentiating students' independent activities makes sense if you are also differentiating your phonics instruction. Choosing activities for students to complete that are appropriate for their levels of development will extend their learning and reinforce the skills you've taught. Differentiating will also ensure that they are able to complete activities without your direct support. This improves engagement during independent work time and cuts down on behavior issues.

Nevertheless, it can be challenging to find time to prepare different activities for different groups of students. In this chapter, we will focus on simple, sustainable ways that you can differentiate students' independent phonics activities, without spending your nights and weekends preparing materials!

Systems for Differentiating Independent Work Activities

Before we look at *what* specific activities you might choose, let's put your mind at ease about the *how*.

First, you'll need to have a system for providing students with the correct materials. There are many different ways to accomplish this. For example, you might designate a color for each of your phonics small groups and obtain folders with these same colors. Students in the blue group would pull activities from the purple folder, and so on (see Figure 9.1). This works well if you have physical centers or stations around the room that students visit. Some of the centers or stations might have three different colored folders, and students are taught to choose an activity from the folder that corresponds to their group's color.

Another option is to designate an independent work folder for each of your students. As you provide students with materials during teacher-led instructional activities (e.g., word lists, decodable texts), students place those materials in their folders for future reuse in centers. You can also add additional activities for students to complete by handing them the materials during small-group instruction, or by preloading folders with activities. If you plan to add activities to each student's folder individually, consider asking a volunteer or assistant for help! Also, even if students have individual work folders, keep in mind that many students in your class might be able to complete the same activity, depending on their levels.

Second, you'll need a plan for teaching students how to complete the activities. Certain activities can be taught to the entire class at the same time and reused throughout the year (for example, rereading a list of words or a decodable text, building words with magnetic letters). Sometimes you'll choose activities that are specific to a group of students. These activities are best taught and practiced ahead of time in a small-group setting.

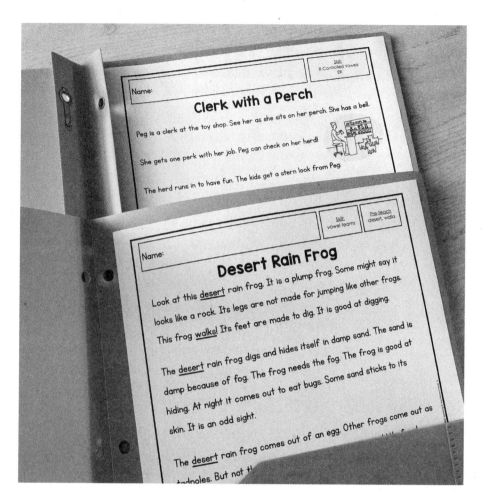

FIGURE 9.1 Differentiated work folders.

Ideas for Differentiated Work Activities

There are endless options for possible phonics activities! An internet search or quick scroll on social media will fill your mind with possibilities. Yet not all activities are equally valuable. Stay focused on the important principles about effective phonics instruction, found in Chapter 2, as you select activities. Look for activities that align with your scope and sequence so that students are not, for example, introduced to consonant blends when they are still trying to master CVC (consonant-vowel-consonant) words. Incorporate a combination of activities to address out-of-context (e.g., reading or building lists of words) and in-context phonics instruction (e.g., reading decodable texts). Help students acquire general word knowledge with tasks that emphasize patterns (e.g., word sorts) rather than rote copying of words (e.g., rainbow writing). Facilitate students' specific word knowledge by including activities to reinforce high-frequency words, irregularly spelled words, and other high-utility words. Also, remember that the simpler you can keep the activities, the easier it is for you to consistently differentiate, and the more likely it is that students will remember how to complete the tasks.

With all of this in mind, here are some examples of effective independent practice activities that can be differentiated with relative ease. All resources pictured are found in our phonics program, *From Sounds to Spelling*, but the concepts can easily be re-created. This is, by no means, an exhaustive list of activities, but simply some ideas to get you started!

Sorting or Resorting Pictures

Picture sorts like the ones in Figure 9.2 are helpful for developing important phonemic awareness skills like isolating and matching the first, final, or vowel sound in a word. They are often used in kindergarten and first grade, but they might be helpful for any reader who is working on mastering these skills. When assigning a picture sort for your students to complete independently, make sure that students have already seen you model how to name each picture out loud, isolate the appropriate sound, and sort it correctly. Teach students how to read down the sort once they are finished by naming the pictures in each column aloud. You might have them do this with a partner for accountability and feedback. Additionally, make sure to choose pictures that students can easily identify, and review the names of the pictures prior to assigning the sort.

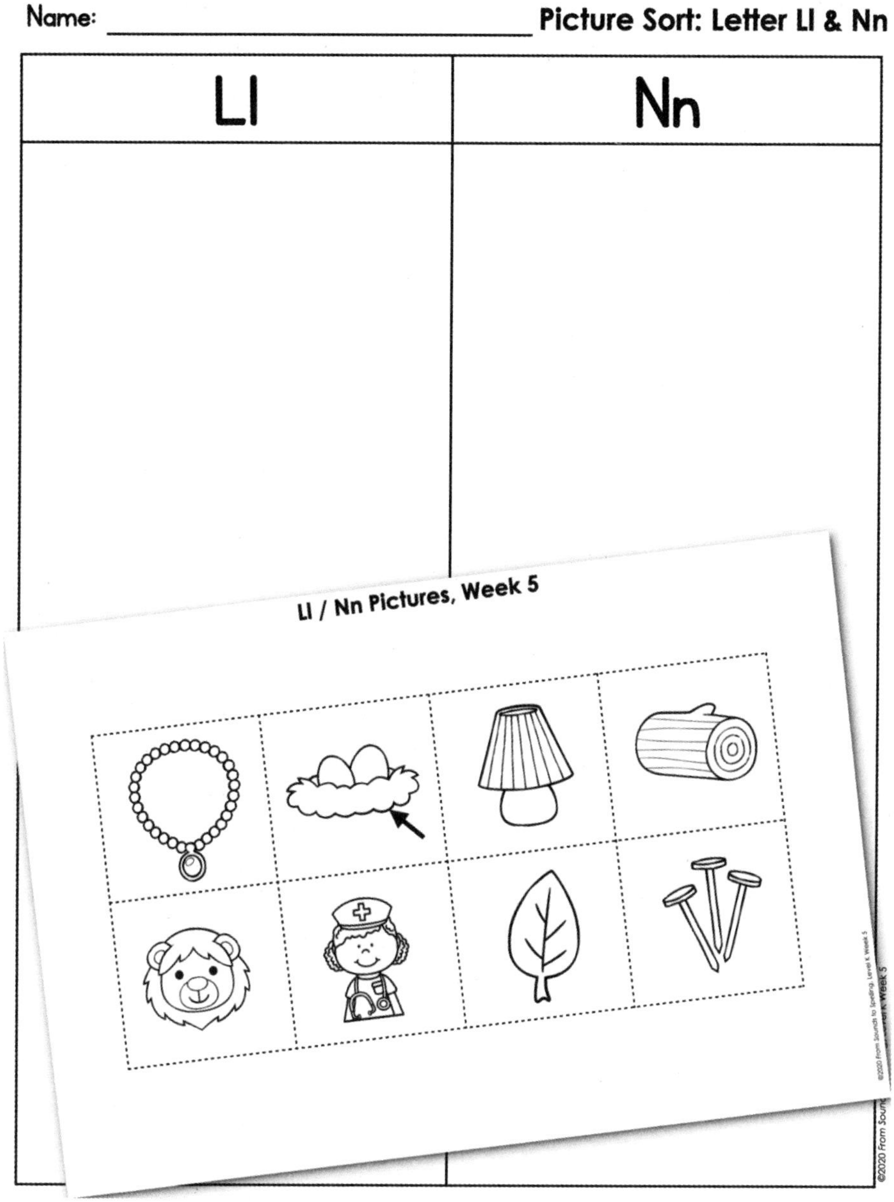

Name: _____ Picture Sort: Letter Ll & Nn

Ll	Nn

Ll / Nn Pictures, Week 5

FIGURE 9.2 Example picture sort.

You can differentiate a picture sort activity by giving students different sorts (e.g., some students sort pictures by their beginning sound and others by their ending sound). Another option is to give some students more pictures to sort than others. Additionally, you might ask students to use phonetic spelling to write a word for some or all of the pictures in the sort; students will produce what they are able to, given their current level of development.

Completing Alphabet Matching Puzzles

Puzzles (wooden, plastic, or printed) are a great practice tool for children learning the alphabet. Some children might need practice matching capital to lowercase letters. Other children might be working on initial sounds and can match alphabet letters to pictures.

Reading or Rereading Word Lists

Any list of words that you use during whole-group or small-group instruction can be reread as an independent activity. This gives students an opportunity to practice their decoding skills and build fluency with the words. Students can read their lists to themselves, video or audio record their reading (for your review at a later time), or read with a partner.

If you provide students with a new list of words rather than having them reread a previously used list, make sure that students have achieved some level of proficiency with all phonics patterns represented on the list. Include review words, and consider mixing similar phonics patterns once students have achieved some proficiency in each individual pattern. Blending lines like the one in Figure 9.3 provide an opportunity for students to briefly review what they already know (short vowels) and practice reading long vowels spelled with silent *e*.

For variety, students might highlight a target phonics pattern prior to reading the list. Or, if there are at least two different phonics patterns represented in the word list, you might have students copy the words

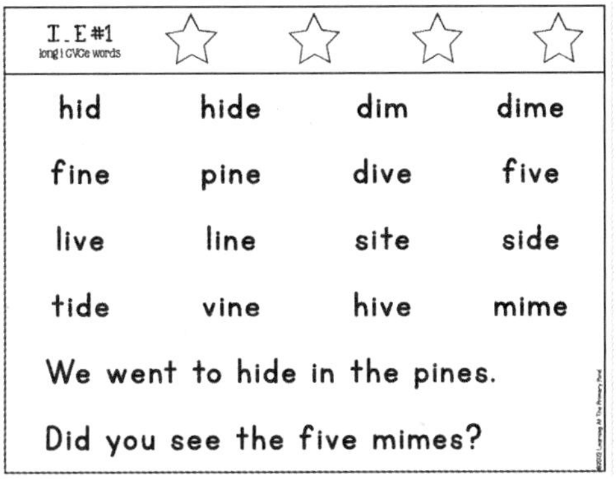

FIGURE 9.3 Example blending line.

I.E #1 long i CVCe words	☆	☆	☆	☆
hid	hide	dim	dime
fine	pine	dive	five
live	line	site	side
tide	vine	hive	mime

We went to hide in the pines.

Did you see the five mimes?

over into two columns after they finish reading them. For example, if the list contains short *o* and long *o* words, you could provide students with two-column paper labeled "short *o*" and "long *o*" (perhaps with example words at the top of the columns), and students copy the words from the list into the appropriate column.

Different groups of children can be given different word lists to use. These lists can vary in length, word complexity (e.g., long vowel words with and without blends) and number of syllables in the words. You might also choose to include a few sentences with the target skill, high-frequency words, and other review words.

Sorting or Resorting Word Cards

As we discussed in Chapter 2, a word sort can easily be completed more than once, as long as students do not glue down the words. Word sorts help students notice patterns. However, make sure that students are reading aloud their words (preferably to a partner) before/during the sort, as well as after the sort. Otherwise, they might end up quickly scanning each word for a pattern and sorting it without actually decoding the words.

Just like word lists, word sorts are relatively easy to differentiate because you can give different sorts to different groups of students. You can also add a fun theme for variety, as shown in Figure 9.4.

FIGURE 9.4 Spring-themed word sort.

Building or Writing Words

Having students spell words is another great independent activity that can easily be differentiated. Just like with the aforementioned activities, different groups of students can spell different words that match the specific skill(s) that they are working on. Always make sure that students have had opportunities to practice spelling words with a target phonics skill with your support (e.g., during a lesson) before you ask them to do this independently.

There are many different activities that can be used for spelling practice. You can have students physically write words and/or build them with magnetic letters or another manipulative. Figure 9.5 shows a say, tap, write activity. Students say the name of the picture aloud, tap one dot as they say each sound in the word, and then write the word into the sound boxes. The dots help students remember to segment the word before attempting to write it. Students might check their work with a partner and/or you can provide them with a word list to check their work after they are finished.

FIGURE 9.5 Say, tap, write activity.

Partner or Small-Group Games

Games are a fun way to have students practice what they are learning! There are endless phonics games available. Look for games that match the skill(s) students are learning. You might choose some games that cover specific phonics patterns and some that address high-frequency words. Many games require that students read words, but you can also add spelling element by having students use a recording sheet to write the words that they land on and read.

If you'd like different groups of students to play different games, make sure to organize your independent work time and space so that students from the same level or small group can play the game together. You could also seek out editable games, like some of those included in *From Sounds to Spelling*, so that you can teach all students the same game directions but have different groups of students practice different words on the game board.

Reading or Rereading Decodable Texts

Students benefit from reading decodable texts more than once, and independent practice time is a great time to fit in additional rereads. This builds fluency and confidence because students feel reading becoming easier each time they reread a text. Students can reread texts independently, with or to a partner, or even record themselves reading. To help students make connections between the phonics skills and high-frequency words you're teaching and the decodable texts they're reading, have students highlight, underline, or make a list of target words before or after they reread the text.

If students will be reading a decodable text for the first time as an independent activity, check to make sure that the text matches your scope and sequence and does not include words with phonics skills that students have not yet been taught. Struggling through lots of challenging words beyond students' level does not result in productive practice time.

Writing About Decodable Texts

Students can extend their work with decodable texts by writing about them. You might have a simple question for students to answer or a generic format for them to follow (e.g., writing about the beginning, middle, and end, or writing three important facts shared in the text). Writing gives students an opportunity to practice spelling target words from the decodable text, as well as work on ideas, sentence structure, spacing, capitalization, and punctuation.

You might provide different writing prompts for different groups of students to answer, or a greater number of writing prompts for certain groups to respond to. Generally speaking, writing is a somewhat self-differentiating activity, because students will only produce what they are able to. For some students, this might be drawing and labeling a picture, and for others, it might be writing paragraphs.

Again, the independent activities described here are simple but effective. There are many wonderful activities available for phonics, but keep in mind the key principles of high-quality phonics instruction when you make selections. Also, remember that kids often enjoy very simple activities. You can easily add variety by offering a choice of writing tools (e.g., colored pencils or markers) or a simple theme (e.g., adding snowflake clip-art to word sort cards to celebrate winter). Sometimes we make preparing independent activities harder or more complicated than it needs to be!

Conclusion

Throughout this book, I've shared a wide range of ideas about how you might use differentiation to meet students' individual needs. That said, I know firsthand what it's like to be a teacher, overwhelmed with ever-increasing demands, trying to figure out how to help 20 or more unique students. To say that teaching is not easy is a *huge* understatement.

I also know that if you read this book, you have a deep desire to help students achieve their full potential. You believe in the power you hold as a teacher to guide your students along their journeys to become proficient readers and writers. You see your students' diverse needs and want to do all that you can to help each child be successful.

Sometimes our efforts to make a difference for our students do not turn out the way we'd like them to. We have the best intentions and plans to try out all these new strategies. At times, we contribute to our own overwhelm because we want to do *so much*. Then, the school year gets busy, we have things going on in our personal lives, and we don't end up implementing what we set out to do.

Not fully following through on our intentions is normal, and something I relate to. What works well for me, however, is to focus on small, sustainable changes. Even though my mind might be bursting with ideas and activities to try, I intentionally limit myself to one or two specific areas. I write down my goals and revisit them every week. I do my best to stay focused. If I think of or read about other new ideas, I write them down to try out at a later time.

After you select one of the differentiation models in this book, try to ease into it. Perhaps you begin small-group phonics instruction, but you intentionally keep your small-group activities limited and brief at first. Or perhaps you use whole-group instruction and want to add some differentiation tools, but you begin with only a single resource like leveled word sorts. If you're like me, you're tempted to do *everything all at once*, but you will likely find that making small changes, one at a time, is more sustainable than implementing multiple major changes simultaneously.

Thank you so much for allowing me to be a little part of your educational journey by reading this book. I would love to keep in touch, and you can find me at `learningattheprimarypond.com`, or @learnin gattheprimarypond on YouTube and other social channels. You can find our phonics program at `fromsoundstospelling.com`.

From the bottom of my heart, thank you for all you do for education and children!

All my best,

Alison

Diagnostic Phonics Assessment

Teacher Directions, p. 1

The purpose of this assessment is to show you which phonics skills students have mastered and which skills they still need to work on. In this appendix, you'll find individual scoring sheets, one per student. If you would like to print class composite sheets, you can access them for free at fromsoundstospelling.com/book.

Part 1: Letter Sounds Assessment

If students are still working on mastering letter sounds or have not yet mastered CVC words, begin here. Otherwise, you can skip this portion.

This is a one-on-one assessment. Follow these directions:

1. Sit at a table with the child. Place the page of lowercase letters in front of the child. Keep the student results sheet in front of you. You will also need a pencil for scoring.

2. Say, "Let's see if you know the sounds of any of these letters." Point to s. "What is the sound of this letter?"
   - If the child says the <u>sound</u> of the letter, nod. (Score it correct on the results sheet.)
   - If the child says the <u>name</u> of the letter, say, "That's a letter name — do you know the <u>sound</u> of the letter?" (Score it correct on the grid below only if they then tell you the letter name on their second try.) If the child says "I don't know" or gives another incorrect response, tell them, "The sound for this letter is / s/." (Score it incorrect.)
   - If the child says a letter <u>sound</u> for a <u>different</u> letter, nod and keep your eyes on your paper. (Score it incorrect on the results sheet.)

4. Continue, moving onto the next letter (m). Don't give any prompts or feedback. Keep your eyes on your paper / the student sheet so the child is not looking to you for feedback. Keep the child moving left to right, top to bottom.

5. If the child becomes frustrated, reassure them that it's okay. If you get through two rows and they do not get any letter sounds correct, point to the rest of the page and ask, "Do you see any letters here that you know?" If not, discontinue the assessment and count all the letters as incorrect.

Part 2: Word Reading Assessment

This is a one-on-one assessment. Follow these directions:

1. Sit at a table with the child. Place the first page of the diagnostic word reading list in front of the child. Keep the student results sheet in front of you. You will also need a pencil for scoring. (You can also use a sheet of blank paper to uncover just one row of words at a time, if you think it will be helpful to keep the child focused.)

2. Say, "I want you to read these words to me. If you don't know a word right away, sound it out. Do your best, but there might be some words that you can't figure out—that's okay! When we are all finished with the assessment, if you want me to read you the tricky words, I will."

3. Have the child begin reading the words to you, moving from left to right. If the child looks at you or says "I don't know," encourage them to sound out the word. Use a checkmark to indicate if a child read a word correctly. Use a dash to indicate a word that the child did not read at all. If a child misreads a word, write down what they said instead of the actual word. You should not indicate to the child when they get a word wrong during the assessment. You can provide encouragement like, "You're doing well; keep going!" if needed.

4. Continue with the assessment until the child misses five words in a row, or if they are becoming visibly frustrated.

Diagnostic Phonics Assessment

Teacher Directions, p. 2

Part 3: Spelling Test

This assessment can be given in a whole-class, small-group, or one-on-one setting. Follow these directions:

1. Give each child blank, lined paper. You will need to have the Teacher Directions sheet available to read from.

2. Explain to students, "I have a list of words that I'd like you to spell. If you know how to spell a word right away, write it. If you're not sure, listen for the sounds in the word and spell those sounds. Some of the words will be tricky, and that's okay—just do your best. You are not getting a grade on this."

3. Begin reading the list of words to students, one by one. Use the provided sentences and have students verbally repeat each word before they spell it.

4. After students have finished writing each word, move on to the next one.

5. Continue until you notice that all students have misspelled at least five words in a row.

6. After you have collected students' papers, you can score them using the student results sheets. If a student got a word correct, use a checkmark. If they got it incorrect, note what they wrote instead. Do not count letter reversals (e.g., "b" for "d") as incorrect spellings.

Analyzing Results

Your results will give you valuable information that you can use to make instructional and grouping decisions. Keep in mind that the word reading and spelling tests will not have covered every possible word (for example, not all vowel teams were tested). However, this will still give you a good starting point.

When making instructional decisions and grouping choices, look closely at the underlined parts of words on the results sheets. Underlining indicates the target part of the word, the skill that was being tested. For example, if students missed the "pl" blend in "ploy" but got the "oy" underlined part correct, this tells you that they have likely mastered this diphthong. If no part of the word is underlined, this means that you should expect the child to have correctly spelled the full word in order to have demonstrated mastery on the skill set.

Diagnostic Phonics Assessment

Individual Student Results Sheet, p. 1

Student:

Date(s):

Letter Sounds

s	m	r	a	l	f	o	n	c	b	x	p	j

g	h	u	t	i	d	y	k	v	z	qu	e	w

Word Reading

1. CVC WORDS

sat	
hem	
fig	
rod	
nets	
subs	

2. DIGRAPHS

chum	
dash	
thin	
whim	
quack	

3. DOUBLE FINAL CONSONANTS

buzz	
moss	
wall	

4. BLENDS

snag	
fled	
drip	

loft	
damp	
flint	

5. GLUED SOUNDS

ping	
plunk	
fang	

6. R-CONTROLLED A, O

| cord | |
| spark | |

7. SILENT E

woke	
gaze	
swipe	
tunes	

8. –ING, –ED ENDINGS

milling	
stamped	
grilled	

9. VOWEL TEAMS

| leak | |

rail	
croak	
gray	
dew	
slight	

10. R-CONTROLLED, ALL

stern	
firm	
pair	
hire	
clear	
pliers	

11. DIPHTHONGS + OO

proud	
thaw	
moist	
hood	
gloom	

12. COMPLEX CONSONANTS

| knee | |

stream	
wren	
peach	
ridge	
splash	
cage	
pitch	

13. BASE WORD CHANGE + ENDING

clipping	
grading	
chided	

14. SCHWA

cattle	
amaze	
happen	
breakable	

15. GREEK AND LATIN ROOTS

generate	
eruption	
pedestrian	
judgmental	

Diagnostic Phonics Assessment

Individual Student Results Sheet, p. 2

Student:

Date(s):

Word Spelling

1. CVC WORDS

sap	
wed	
rot	
fin	
lug	
pits	

2. DIGRAPHS

po<u>sh</u>	
<u>ch</u>ug	
tu<u>ck</u>	

3. DOUBLE FINAL CONSONANTS

hi<u>ss</u>	
ha<u>ll</u>	

4. BLENDS

<u>sm</u>og	
<u>cl</u>ad	
<u>tr</u>am	
pe<u>nt</u>	
<u>cr</u>a<u>mp</u>	

5. GLUED SOUNDS

to<u>ng</u>	
pli<u>nk</u>	

6. R-CONTROLLED A, O

d<u>ar</u>t	
h<u>or</u>n	

7. SILENT E

d<u>i</u>n<u>e</u>	
dr<u>o</u>v<u>e</u>	
t<u>u</u>b<u>e</u>	

8. -ING, -ED ENDINGS

send<u>ing</u>	
fix<u>ed</u>	

9. VOWEL TEAMS

m<u>ai</u>n	
br<u>igh</u>t	
f<u>oa</u>m	
st<u>ee</u>p	

10. R-CONTROLLED, ALL

p<u>er</u>ch	
b<u>oar</u>d	
st<u>ir</u>	
p<u>ur</u>se	
st<u>air</u>s	

11. DIPHTHONGS + OO

c<u>oi</u>n	
br<u>ow</u>	
pl<u>oy</u>	
st<u>oo</u>d	

12. COMPLEX CONSONANTS

<u>spr</u>ay	

<u>gn</u>at	
ba<u>dge</u>	
sli<u>ce</u>	
ra<u>ge</u>	
<u>batch</u>	

13. BASE WORD CHANGE + ENDING

slamming	
faded	
wading	

14. SCHWA

rubble	
amount	
legal	
ignorant	

15. GREEK AND LATIN ROOTS

credible	
vision	
corporation	

Letter Sounds Diagnostic

s	m	r	a
l	f	o	n
c	b	x	p
j	g	h	u
t	i	d	y
k	v	z	qu
e	w		

Diagnostic Word Reading (p. 1)

sat	hem	fig	rod
nets	subs	chum	dash
thin	whim	quack	buzz
moss	wall	snag	fled
drip	loft	damp	flint
ping	plunk	fang	cord
spark	woke	gaze	swipe
tunes	milling	stamped	grilled
leak	rail	croak	gray

Diagnostic Word Reading (p. 2)

dew	slight	stern	firm
pair	hire	clear	pliers
proud	thaw	moist	hood
gloom	knee	stream	wren
peach	ridge	splash	cage
pitch	clipping	grading	chided
cattle	amaze	happen	breakable
generate	eruption	pedestrian	judgmental

Diagnostic Spelling Test
Teacher Directions, p. 1

Have your student(s) number a piece of paper (start with 1–10, and they can add more later as needed). Read this list of words, one at a time. (If students are reading at a second grade level or higher, you can skip the first five words.) Make sure to read the example sentence before students begin spelling each word. When giving the assessment, use each word in a sentence. Feel free to allow students to take breaks, or to give this test over two sessions if needed. You can stop when students have misspelled five words in a row.

1. sap – The sap from the tree felt sticky.
2. wed – If two people get married, we say that they were wed.
3. rot – If we leave the food out for too long, it will rot.
4. fin – The fish has a tiny fin.
5. lug – To lug something is to carry something heavy, dragging it along.
6. pits – Peaches and plums have pits in the center.
7. posh – If something is very fancy, we can say that it is posh.
8. chug – To chug something is to drink a lot of it quickly.
9. tuck – When I was young, I liked it when my parents would tuck me in.
10. hiss – Did you hear the cat hiss loudly?
11. hall – We walked down the hall to another classroom.
12. smog – Smog is a type of air pollution that looks like dirty fog.
13. clad – To be clad in something means to be wearing it.
14. tram – Some people call a trolley car a tram.
15. pent – If you haven't gotten to play outside for a while, you might have a lot of pent up energy.
16. cramp – I got a cramp in my side when I was running.
17. tong – A tong in the pair was broken.
18. plink – The rain fell plink, plink on our roof.
19. dart – She threw a dart at the dart board.
20. horn – A horn can be a musical instrument or something that you honk on the steering wheel of your car.
21. dine – We decided to dine on roast chicken and broccoli.
22. drove – We drove for a long time to get to the museum.
23. tube – Toothpaste sometimes comes in a tube.
24. sending – I am sending you a letter in the mail.
25. fixed – Mom fixed the broken fridge.
26. main – Main street was busy yesterday.
27. bright – The sun was very bright the other day.
28. foam – If you wash your hands well, the soap will make a foam.
29. steep – The mountain we drove up was very steep.

Diagnostic Spelling Test

30. perch - The bird likes to sit on her <u>perch</u>.
31. board - The deck was missing a <u>board</u>.
32. stir - Please <u>stir</u> the pancake mix with a spoon.
33. purse - I left my <u>purse</u> in the trunk of the car.
34. stairs - He climbed the <u>stairs</u> slowly.
35. coin - I found a <u>coin</u> in my pocket.
36. brow - Another word for a person's forehead is their <u>brow</u>.
37. ploy - Asking for help was a <u>ploy</u> to distract the man, so the criminal could grab his wallet.
38. stood - We <u>stood</u> in line for a long time.
39. spray - The flowers need to be watered with a <u>spray</u> of the hose.
40. gnat - A <u>gnat</u> is a small insect.
41. badge - The police officer lost her <u>badge</u>.
42. slice - Can I have a <u>slice</u> of pizza?
43. rage - <u>Rage</u> is a feeling of intense anger.
44. batch - We made a big <u>batch</u> of cookies.
45. slamming - <u>Slamming</u> your toy down may cause it to break.
46. faded - The sun <u>faded</u> the pillow color on our outdoor couch.
47. wading - We are <u>wading</u> in the ocean, but we won't get all the way in yet.
48. rubble - After the building burned down, the firefighters searched through the <u>rubble</u> that was left.
49. amount - You do not have the right <u>amount</u> of money to purchase this game.
50. legal - Something that is <u>legal</u> does not break the law.
51. ignorant - If you are <u>ignorant</u> of something, that means you do not know it.
52. credible - We found the speaker to be very <u>credible</u>, so we believed him.
53. vision - You can get your <u>vision</u> checked at the eye doctor.
54. corporation - A <u>corporation</u> is one type of business.

Index